Booktalks and Beyond

Thematic Activities
for Grades K–6

Nancy J. Keane

UpstartBooks
Fort Atkinson, WI

To my children, Aureta and Alex Keane
And to the memory of my mother, Aureta C. Keane

Acknowledgments

I wish to thank the people who have helped with this endeavor. First, the authors need to be thanked. With so many marvelous children's books in print, it was quite difficult to limit the entries in this book. Without these extraordinary people, this would have been a thankless task. As it was, I have spent numerous entertaining hours wrapped up in wonderful books.

I would also like to thank the many librarians I have come in contact with. They have introduced me to books I may have missed. The library staff of the Concord (N.H.) School District has been very helpful—especially when I begged to borrow books from their collections. The staff of the Children's Room at Concord (N.H.) Public Library has also been helpful. Their fantastic collection kept me ensconced in quality literature for many, many days.

The many wonderful, dedicated teachers I have had the privilege of knowing also influenced this work tremendously. Their ideas for activities and their willingness to share have helped a great deal. I have been fortunate to work with a talented group of educators.

I would like to thank Matt Mulder from UpstartBooks for his commitment to this project. Truly, without him, this would not be possible. His ideas and comments really helped shape this work. Virginia Harrison from UpstartBooks had the daunting task of editing the manuscript.

Most importantly, I would like to thank my family. My children Aureta and Alex didn't complain too much about the amount of time I spent in the library or on the computer. They listened to the books I read to them and gave me their opinions on them. If you really want to know if a child will like a book, ask a child. My children are the best!

Published by Upstart Books
W5527 Highway 106
P.O. Box 800
Fort Atkinson, Wisconsin 53538-0800
1-800-558-2110

© Nancy J. Keane, 2001
Cover by Debra Neu Sletten

The paper used in this publication meets the minimum requirements of American National Standard for Information Science — Permanence of Paper for Printed Library Material. ANSI/NISO Z39.48-1992.

 Contents

Introduction

The stories in children's literature reflect society and help children learn about their world. Children's literature shows different perspectives from which children may experience events in a non-threatening way. For instance, historical fiction introduces them to what life was like long ago, and it is accessible because it is told in a way that is understandable to young children. By introducing children to different concepts via fiction, we open the door to expand the exploration of topics in greater depth.

One way to excite children about reading is to use booktalks. Booktalks are short promos that tease children into wanting to know more. Books that are not promoted often stay on the shelves to collect dust. When children hear about books either through friends or though booktalks, they are more apt to read them.

The purpose of this book is to promote fiction reading and to encourage the discussion to go further into real-life activities. Each chapter is divided into two age groups. The first is geared toward children in kindergarten through grade three. Most of the books listed there are picture books. The second part of each chapter is geared toward children in grades four through six. These books are for more independent readers.

Each topical section offers sample booktalks, a list of books reflecting the topic, and activities that can bring that topic further into the child's day-to-day life.

The booktalks can be modified to reflect the needs of the population of children and the style of the booktalker. Each booktalk listing includes author, title, publisher, date of publication, interest level (IL) and reading level (RL). Both levels indicate grades.

The book lists suggest books that reflect the chapter's theme. Every entry in the book list provides the book's author, title, publisher, date of publication, interest level and reading level. There is also a short annotation based on the book's Library of Congress summary statement.

Activities for the particular age group follow the book list. These are suggestions for things you may want to do with your students to follow up on the theme. They are just starters, and they leave plenty of room for you to personalize the activity.

I hope that this book will inspire teachers, school librarians and public librarians to use booktalking as a starting point for discussions of themes. When children begin a lesson with enthusiasm, it's sure to be a hit.

To find out more about booktalking and to access a database of ready-to-use booktalks, visit the author's web page, *Booktalks—Quick and Simple*, at www.nancykeane.com. The author has also set up a listserv to share and discuss booktalks. To join, simply visit *Booktalks—Quick and Simple* and click on "Click to subscribe to booktalkers."

How to Booktalk

Booktalking can be a rewarding experience for both the adult and the child. The enthusiasm can be infectious. The reward is connecting children to books.

What Exactly Is a Booktalk?

A booktalk is like a movie trailer. The idea is to "sell" the book. You want to give enough information to tease the audience into wanting more.

Is a Booktalk Like a Book Review?

No. A booktalk is not a review. You don't need to say whether you liked the book or not. It is assumed that it is worth reading because you are promoting it. You can say you found it amusing or entertaining, but you really don't need to say how you feel about the book.

Do's and Don'ts of Booktalking

There are definitely some guidelines that can help your booktalking. However, remember that nothing is written in stone. Your booktalks should reflect your own style and personality. Be sure to gear your booktalks to your audience.

Do

- Bring the books with you. It helps create enthusiasm if the children can see the book. If that is not possible, you can substitute a color copy of the cover or a color overhead transparency so that the children can at least see the cover.

- Memorize the booktalks. This gives a spontaneous, connected feel to the presentation. If you cannot memorize the booktalks, have a cheat sheet with you that you hide behind the book, and refer to it only as needed.

- Vary themes. If you are talking about one theme, vary the type of book: one humorous, one serious—one upbeat, one dark.

- Keep records of books used. This is particularly important if you booktalk to the same group more than once. You don't want to keep repeating yourself.

- Be prepared to ad lib. Don't be afraid to vary from the script. You may find that you can relate a talk to a particular group in a way that you didn't anticipate.

- Vary the length of the booktalks. It breaks up the presentation and is much more interesting. You might want to include one-line descriptions of books between the booktalks.

- Start strong and end strong. Choose a really dynamic booktalk to end your presentation. Leave them wanting more.

- Have realistic expectations. Some booktalks will create more enthusiasm than others. Sometimes children just aren't in the mood to listen.

- Be organized, cool and confident. Show that you know the books and want the children to read them too.

- Relax and enjoy. Have fun with it.

- Learn from your mistakes. If a booktalk bombs, rethink it and rewrite it.

Don't

- Booktalk books you haven't read. It will show. You may lose your credibility with the children.

- Booktalk books you didn't like. Again, children will pick up on it—or if they choose the book based on your booktalk and they don't like it either, your credibility will be questioned.

- Gush. Too much enthusiasm sounds phony.

- Give away the ending or any major surprises. Why would anyone bother to read a book if they know how it ends?

- Give a book review. That is a different presentation altogether. Booktalks are just advertisements for books. They are not reports on the books' literary merit.

- Label by gender/race/other, such as "these books are just for boys." Each book can be enjoyed by anyone.

- Oversell. Again, you'll sound phony. You also risk setting up false expectations in the minds of the children.

- Read from the book unless you have to. Sometimes you want to give the flavor of the writing style, but usually you should try to stay away from reading.

- Talk about sex, drugs or violence without first clearing your booktalk with teachers and parents. There are times to bring up controversial topics in schools, but be sure that this is one of those times.

- Booktalk books you don't own. It is very frustrating for children to hear about a book only to find that they don't have access to it.

- Bore yourself. If you feel boring to yourself, imagine how the audience feels.

- Start booktalks with booktalks. Always introduce the topic/theme first and tell the children a little of what they can expect to hear in the next few minutes.

Types of Booktalks

There is no set booktalk style. Here are a few basic types of booktalks.

- Brief summary of book. Give a summary of the book, leaving the ending out. You may end the booktalk with a question or a challenge for the child to guess how the book ends.

- Concentrate on a character from the book. This is usually a major character, but you can also use a minor character that the child will meet in the books. You can:

  - Do the booktalk from that character's perspective.

  - Talk about the character as if it's someone you know.

  - Ask the children if they would like the character as a friend.

- Make comparisons to other books. The book that you use for comparison should be one that the children might have read or heard about.

- Discuss the author's purpose in writing this book.

- Describe an event in the author's life that influenced the writing of this book.

- Compare events in the book to your own life. How is this story similar or different? You may also compare events in the book to something that's familiar to the children.

- Share a favorite event/scene from the book and tell why it is your favorite.

Hooks for Books

Try some of these techniques when booktalking.

- *Audience participation.* Get the audience involved.Children can repeat an expression from the book. Ask questions of the audience before you go into the booktalk to get them involved.

- *Surprise.* Start with just a list of dry facts—then jump to a shocking or exciting event.

- *Headlines.* Refer to an article in the news and then relate it to the book you are talking. To show the connection, you may bring in a newspaper and pretend you are reading it.

- *Jump cut.* Jump quickly from one scene to another—let the audience deduce the connection.

- *O. Henry.* Set up one set of expectations, and then pull the rug out from under your audience.

- *Questions.* Ask a series of questions to set the mood or to pique curiosity.

- *Sounds and props.* For sounds, clap your hands, snap your fingers, or stamp your foot. As for props, you can use a real object or just pantomime the object—e.g., lighting a candle.

- *Themes.* Talk about several books that share the same theme.

- *What if?* Present the moral dilemma facing the central character.

- *You.* Relate the events in the book to events in the listeners' lives.

And Finally...

The number one rule of booktalking is to have fun and not worry about all the other rules!

Author Autobiographies

Everyone has a story—the story of his or her life. When authors write books, they often draw on their own lives for ideas. These books are all based on the authors' lives. They give children insight into what inspired the author to write a particular story. It is hoped that reading about an author's life will inspire children to become more observant in their own lives.

Booktalks (Grades K–3)

Once Upon a Time

Bunting, Eve; photographs by John Pezaris. Richard C. Owen Publishers, 1995. (IL K–3, RL 4.1)

Eve Bunting was born in Ireland. She moved to California back in the 1950s with her husband and children. It is there that she decided to try to be a writer. She set up an office in the attic of their house and warned her children not to bother her unless it was an emergency. Of course, you know that everything is an emergency to a kid, right? Well, her kids were no different. In spite of the interruptions, Eve Bunting wrote her first book about an Irish giant named Finn MacCool. After her first success, she began writing more and more, which is great for us because she has written so many good books! Find out about her life in *Once Upon a Time*.

Bigmama's

Crews, Donald. Morrow, 1991. (IL K–3, RL 2.2)

Summer at Grandma's house. Is there anything like it? This book recalls Grandma's old treadle sewing machine, her wind-up record player and the chicken coop that held Sunday's dinner. There are aunts and uncles and cousins everywhere. This is a wonderful book full of lots of great memories. Learn more about the author's childhood in *Bigmama's* by Donald Crews.

Surprising Myself

Fritz, Jean; photographs by Andrea Fritz Pfleger. Richard C. Owen Publishers, 1992. (IL K–3, RL 4.4)

Have you ever known someone who grew up in a different country? Well, Jean Fritz grew up in China. She lives in New York now. She loved to explore the Yangtse River in China as a child. She loves to explore even further as an adult. She tells us how she gets her ideas for her books and how she goes about writing them. When she leaves her home she is worried that her unfinished manuscripts might get ruined, so she puts them in the safest place she can think of. Can you guess where that might be? The refrigerator! Find out more about Jean Fritz in her book *Surprising Myself*.

My Mysterious World

Mahy, Margaret; photographs by David Alexander. Richard C. Owen Publishers, 1995. (IL K–3, RL 4.5)

Children's author Margaret Mahy invites us into her life. This book is filled with photographs of the author as well as insights into her working style. She rises well before the sun comes up to start her day. She takes her writing very seriously and stays on schedule. She lives in New Zealand and often walks along the shore to come up with ideas or to figure out what to write next. Visit with Margaret Mahy and find out about *My Mysterious World*.

A Letter from Phoenix Farm

Yolen, Jane; photographs by Jason Stemple. Richard C. Owen Publishers, 1992. (IL K–3, RL 4.9)

Jane Yolen has written hundreds of children's books. She lives on a farm in western Massachusetts and invites us to explore her life. She shows us the office in the attic of her home where she does her writing. We also learn about her other pursuits, such as editing, and leading a discussion group for people who want to write for children. Find out some of the things that have led to stories in *A Letter from Phoenix Farm*.

Booktalks (Grades 4–6)

A Writer's Story: From Life to Fiction

Bauer, Marion Dane. Clarion, 1996. (IL 5–8, RL 7.5)

Well-known children's author Marion Bauer takes you on a journey of her life. She tells how her life has influenced her writing. Throughout the book, she tells young writers how to take what they know and put it into writing. She explains the creative process and takes you through specific aspects of the writing process. Ms. Bauer uses her experience as both a writer and a teacher of writing to answer questions that young writers may have.

Boy

Dahl, Roald. Farrar, 1984. (IL 5–8, RL 6.4)

The famous author of *James and the Giant Peach* and *Charlie and the Chocolate Factory* tells of his boyhood adventures while attending a boys' boarding school, taking summer trips, and experiencing typical boyhood tricks and punishments. Find out what sweet job he held that made all the other boys jealous. If you want to know about the time he almost lost his nose, read *Boy* by Roald Dahl.

26 Fairmount Avenue

dePaola, Tomie. Putnam, 1999. (IL 3–6, RL 4.8)

Do you remember moving into a new house when you were little? Do you remember how you felt about moving from your familiar surroundings into a brand new home in a brand new neighborhood? Children's author Tomie dePaola certainly does. He tells the story of his family building a brand new house. There are many obstacles to overcome along the way, including the hurricane of 1938 that almost destroyed the half-finished house. Through it all, young Tomie and his family are determined to move into the house at *26 Fairmount Avenue*.

Bill Peet: An Autobiography

Peet, Bill. Houghton Mifflin, 1994. (IL 3–6, RL 6.7)

Have you ever seen the Disney movie "Cinderella"? It is one of my favorites. Have you ever wondered what it takes to create an animated movie? It takes thousands of drawings with just slight changes between the drawings to make the characters seem to move. Bill Peet was a Disney illustrator for years before he started writing children's books. He finally left when he realized that he could not draw one more duck! He then became a story editor and created some of the memorable Disney stories. We are happy that he turned to children's books so that we have met Chester the worldly pig, Cowardly Clyde and many others. In his autobiography, Bill Peet tells us about his childhood and brings us inside the Disney studios. You also will learn how he came up with ideas for his books. Bill Peet uses words and pictures to tell his fascinating life story.

West from Home: Letters of Laura Ingalls Wilder to Almanzo Wilder, San Francisco, 1915

Wilder, Laura Ingalls. Harper & Row, 1974. (IL 5–8, RL 5.5)

You probably know Laura Ingalls Wilder through her Little House on the Prairie series of books. She wrote a total of nine books that told of her life growing up in the latter part of the 19th century. What you may not know is that Laura did not write any of these books until she was in her 60s. This book is a collection of letters that Laura wrote to her husband Almanzo during the fall of 1915. Laura's daughter Rose had moved to San Francisco and was a successful newspaper columnist there. During the fall of 1915, a tremendous World's Fair was being held in San Francisco. The Panama Canal had just opened, and California celebrated with the Panama-Pacific International Exposition. Rose invited her mother to attend this spectacular event. Almanzo stayed on the farm to keep the place going and sent Laura on the journey. Through Laura's daily letters home, we experience the week-long journey to the coast, the people she met along the way, the awe of her first visit to the Pacific Ocean and, of course, her days at the World's Fair. We also learn how Rose convinces her mother to start writing. At first Laura agrees to write for a local newspaper but, as we know, that was just the start of her writing career! Enjoy Laura's trip in *West From Home.*

Asch, Frank. *One Man Show.* Richard C. Owen Publishers, 1997. (IL K–3, RL 2.8) In this autobiographical account, the author/illustrator shares his life, daily activities, and creative process, and shows how all are intertwined.

Cole, Joanna. On the Bus With Joanna Cole: A Creative Autobiography. Heinemann, 1996. (IL K–3, RL 5.9) The author discusses her life, how she came to be a writer, where she gets her ideas, and what is involved in producing a book.

Ehlert, Lois. *Under My Nose.* Richard C. Owen Publishers, 1996. (IL K–3, RL 3.5) An author and illustrator of books for young people, Lois Ehlert shares how she interweaves her creative process with her daily routine.

Haskins, Francine. *I Remember "121."* Children's Book Press, 1991. (IL K–3, RL 4.9) The author describes her family life and daily activities from age 3 to 9 and celebrates the experience of growing up in a traditional African-American community in Washington, D.C.

Hurwitz, Johanna. *A Dream Come True.* Richard C. Owen Publishers, 1998. (IL K–3, RL 4.2) A prominent children's books author shares her life, her daily activities, and her creative process.

Kuskin, Karla. *Thoughts, Pictures, and Words.* Richard C. Owen Publishers, 1995. (IL K–3, RL 4.1) The author shows where she lives and works, recounts her childhood, introduces her family, and explains how she writes.

Lester, Helen. *Author: A True Story.* Houghton Mifflin, 1997. (IL K–3, RL 2.8) Children's author Helen Lester describes her life from age three to adulthood and discusses how she writes.

Lyon, George Ella. *A Sign.* Orchard Books, 1998. (IL K–3, RL 3.5) The author simply describes how she considered various careers as she grew and how she combined them all into her work as a writer.

Polacco, Patricia. *Firetalking.* Richard C. Owen Publishers, 1994. (IL K–3, RL 4.9) The author recounts her life and describes how her daily activities and the writing and drawing processes are interwoven.

Van Leeuwen, Jean. *Growing Ideas.* Richard C. Owen Publishers, 1998. (IL K–3, RL 4.8) The author of the popular books about Oliver and Amanda Pig describes her creative process, her life, and her daily activities.

Ada, Alma Flor. *Under the Royal Palms: A Childhood in Cuba.* Atheneum Books for Young Readers, 1998. (IL 3–6, RL 6.1) The author recalls her life and impressions growing up in Cuba.

Adler, David A. *My Writing Day.* Richard C. Owen Publishers, 1999. (IL 3–6, RL 6.0) The author of many works of both fiction and nonfiction describes his creative process, his daily activities, and his life.

Author Talk: Conversations with Judy Blume...[Et Al]. Simon & Schuster Books for Young Readers, 2000. (IL 3–6, RL 5.3) This volume presents interviews with 15 well-known children's writers, including Judy Blume, Karen Cushman, Russell Freedman, James Howe, Lois Lowry, Gary Paulsen, and Laurence Yep.

Cherry, Lynne. *Making a Difference In the World.* Richard C. Owen Publishers, 2000. (IL 3–6, RL 5.2) A prominent children's book author and illustrator shares her life, her daily activities, her interest in environmental preservation, and her creative process, showing how all are intertwined.

dePaola, Tomie. *Here We All Are.* Putnam, 2000. (IL 3–6, RL 4.6) Children's author-illustrator Tomie dePaola describes his experiences at home and in school when he was a boy.

Gag, Wanda. *The Girlhood Diary of Wanda Gag, 1908–1909: Portrait of a Young Artist.* Blue Earth Books, 2001. (IL 3–6, RL 4.0) The diary of Wanda Gag records her childhood experiences in school, hardships at home, and dreams of becoming a great artist. Includes sidebars, activities, and a timeline related to this era.

Kehret, Peg. *Small Steps: The Year I Got Polio.* A. Whitman, 2000. (IL 3–6, RL 5.6) The author describes her battle against polio when she was 13 and her efforts to overcome its debilitating effects.

McKissack, Pat. *Can You Imagine?* Richard C. Owen Publishers, 1997. (IL 3–6, RL 4.8) The author of the Newbery Honor Book *The Dark Thirty* describes her life, how she became a writer, how her family helps with her writing, and how she gets her ideas.

Naylor, Phyllis Reynolds. *How I Came To Be a Writer.* Simon & Schuster, 2001. (IL 3–6, RL 5.9) This book details Naylor's career from stories she composed in grade school through her first published pieces to novels she's written to date.

Pringle, Laurence P. *Nature! Wild and Wonderful*. Richard C. Owen Publishers, 1997. (IL 3–6, RL 3.5) A prominent children's author shares his life, his daily activities, and his creative process.

Activities (Grades K–3)

- Discuss with students the difference between fiction and nonfiction. Students should know that stories based on factual information are called "nonfiction."

- Have students complete a survey chart introducing themselves to others. Items may include age, hair color, eye color, siblings, favorite things, and so on.

- Students can interview their parents to find out basic information about their birth and childhood.

- Give students the assignment of writing their own autobiographies with details of their memories so far. Students can compile information about their interests and hobbies.

- Have students make drawings and cut pictures from magazines to illustrate the main attributes of the author in the autobiography. Students can make a collage and explain why they chose the various pictures.

Activities (Grades 4–6)

- Have students compile a poster board or scrapbook using photographs and written explanations to tell the stories of their lives from birth to current day. Organize a parent brunch during which parents can see the posters and booklets designed by your students.

- Design a bulletin board called "Look Who's Talking," and have each student bring in one baby picture. Back all pictures with construction paper and a number. Then have the class match each others' names with the numbered pictures.

- Design a "Look Who's Famous" bulletin board. Put up clues about the person your class is studying. Invite students from other classes to come in and try to guess who this famous person is.

- Ask students to give examples of information that could be put into an autobiography. Stress the importance of sticking to highlights and being concise.

- After students read a biography or autobiography, ask them to draw a "Wanted" poster for that person. This allows them to focus on the character.

Bullies

It's an unfortunate fact of life that everyone will encounter a bully at some time. Some of us find ourselves being picked on more than others. Children need to learn why bullying is wrong. They also need to learn strategies for coping with bullying behavior. These books feature bullies and show different approaches to handling the situation.

Booktalks (Grades K–3)

Crickwing

Cannon, Janell. Harcourt, 2000. (IL K–3, RL 3.4)

Crickwing hated his name. All the other cockroaches called him that because his wing was pulled out of place during a close run-in with a toad. While the other cockroaches were gathering their food at night, Crickwing would go off on his own. He liked to play with his food. He would make beautiful sculptures with his meal before he ate it. Usually before Crickwing could enjoy his art, a larger animal would come along and snatch it away from him. Crickwing was tired of being picked on. When he came across a colony of leaf cutter ants, he decided it would be fun to pick on someone smaller for a change. He tripped them, put them on high branches and even dug ant traps for them to fall in. He was having so much fun terrorizing the ants. He became a real bully. The ants decided that they must do something to stop Crickwing. Could these small ants stop such a large cockroach? Can they change Crickwing's attitude? Read *Crickwing* by Janell Cannon to find out.

Black Belt

Faulkner, Matt. Alfred A. Knopf, 2000. (IL K–3, RL 2.2)

Have you ever been bothered by a bully? Young Bushi certainly has. After school, Bushi is confronted by Yag-ya and others who start to pour a soda all over him. When Bushi tries to run away, he accidentally spills the soda over Yag-ya. Bushi runs for his life! He ducks inside a karate school called a dojo and loses the bullies. He notices a black belt hanging up on the wall. He takes it down and tries it on. Suddenly, he is transported back in time and meets the wise master who teaches him much about how to handle bullies. What lessons does Bushi learn that will help him? Will he be able to return to his present life? To find out, read *Black Belt* by Matt Faulkner.

Hooway for Wodney Wat

Lester, Helen; ill. by Lynn Munsinger. Houghton Mifflin, 2000. (IL K–3, RL 2.5)

Wodney Wat has a problem. You see, he is really Rodney Rat, but he can't pronounce his "r's." Every time he says a word that has an "r" in it, it comes out as a "w." The kids at school tease him terribly to the point that he doesn't want to talk. He hides inside his jacket and hopes the teasing will stop. When a new girl enters the class, thing change—for the worse! She is the biggest, meanest bully Wodney has ever seen. He is terrified to speak in front of her because he just knows she will make fun of him. Everyone in the class is afraid of her. When Wodney is chosen to lead the class in a game of Simon Says, an unexpected thing happens. Can you guess what it may be? Join Wodney and the kids of PS142 Elementary School in *Hooway for Wodney Wat.*

King of the Playground

Naylor, Phyllis Reynolds; ill. by Nola Langner Malone. Atheneum, 1991. (IL K–3, RL 3.3)

Kevin gets up in the morning and puts on his Spiderman T-shirt, his Batman underpants and his jeans with the horseshoes on the pockets. He isn't feeling particularly brave, but he is going to go to the playground. If he is really lucky, he'll get there before Sammy gets there. No such luck. Sammy is there. Sammy tells Kevin that he can't play because Sammy is King of the Playground. Sammy threatens to tie Kevin up if he doesn't leave. When Kevin gets home and tells his father about it, his father asks Kevin what he would do if Sammy tried to tie him up. Kevin thought about the time he tried to put a sweater on his cat and realized he could fight back. Day after day, Sammy threatens Kevin. Day after day, Kevin's dad talks to Kevin about the threat. Will Kevin ever get up the courage to stand up to Sammy? Will he regret it? Will he ever be able to confront the *King of the Playground?*

Big Bad Bruce

Peet, Bill. Houghton Mifflin, 1982. (IL K–3, RL 4.1)

Forevergreen Forest was a very peaceful place to live. All the animals loved living there until Bruce moved into the forest. Bruce was a bear who was so big he scared everyone with his size. He also liked to roll boulders down the hill. When he realized how much he scared all the other animals by doing this, he started doing it more often! He loved watching the animals scrambling for safety. One day he found a really big boulder at the top of a hill. He used all his strength to roll the boulder down the hill. On the way, it tore down trees and sent all the animals running for cover. At the bottom of the hill, it barely missed a little old lady and her cat. When she complained to Bruce, he thought it was the funniest thing he had ever seen. He roared with laughter. What Bruce didn't know is that this old woman was really a witch. She was about to turn the tables on Bruce. Can you guess what happens to him? To see what happens, read *Big Bad Bruce* by Bill Peet.

Booktalks (Grades 4–6)

King of the Kooties

Dadey, Debbie. Walker & Co., 1999. (IL 3–6, RL 4.0)

"Eeeuuwww! You have kooties!" Donald didn't quite understand what Louisa means by this, but he could tell by the way the other kids were acting that it wasn't a good thing. It's hard enough to be the new kid in town. It's even harder when you are being teased every day. Donald and his new friend Nate do everything they can think of to stop Louisa, but nothing seems to work. So they decide they must take desperate measures and have no choice but to kill her—with kindness, that is. To find out what happens, read *King of the Kooties* by Debbie Dadey.

Yolanda's Genius

Fenner, Carol. Aladdin, 1995. (IL 3–6, RL 4.2)

Yolanda is smart, tough and big for her age. Her younger brother Andrew loves to play the harmonica. Yolanda believes that he is a real genius even though most people think he is a bit slow. After the family moves from Chicago to Michigan, some school bullies take

Andrew's harmonica, and he retreats into himself. Can Yolanda convince people that there is more to Andrew than they think? Can she replace the prized harmonica and unleash her brother's genius? Read *Yolanda's Genius* to find out.

Stepping on the Cracks
Hahn, Mary Downing. Clarion, 1991. (IL 3–6, RL 6.3)

Have you ever known a bully? Have you gone beyond the bully's behavior and gotten to know the person? This book takes place during World War II. Margaret's older brother is away fighting in the war. Her whole family is worried about him being safe. She really doesn't need to be bothered by Gordy, the class bully. Margaret and her best friend Elizabeth are having their own personal war at school with the school bullies, Gordy, Doug, and Toad. One day, Margaret and Elizabeth find out a secret about Gordy—a secret that can change all their lives. How will the girls deal with what they find out? Will they be able to keep Gordy's secret? Will they be responsible for ruining a life? You will just have to read *Stepping on the Cracks* by Mary Downing Hahn to find out.

Nothing Wrong with a Three-legged Dog
McNamee, Graham. Delacorte Press, 2000. (IL 3–5, RL 4.5)

Fourth grader Keath is in a bad situation. He's a white boy in a predominantly black school. His best friend, Lynda, has a black mother and a white father. The class bully calls Keath "Whitey" and Lynda "Zebra." They are constantly harassed by the other kids—especially by Toothpick, the worst bully of all. Keath thinks his life can't get any worse. Of course, it can! His grandmother suffers a stroke. Keath is afraid to visit her anymore. She looks and speaks differently. What both Keath and Lynda love is dogs. When Keath finds out that a dog is visiting his grandmother in the hospital, Keath decides that he might like to visit after all. How will the dogs affect Keath? The bullies? Will he be able to spend time with his grandmother again? Will the bullies leave him alone? And what's up with that three-legged, one-eared beagle? To find out, read *Nothing Wrong with a Three-legged Dog* by Graham McNamee.

Joshua T. Bates In Trouble Again
Shreve, Susan Richards. Knopf, 1997. (IL 3–6, RL 5.9)

Joshua can't believe he was kept back in third grade. Of course, everyone made fun of him for flunking the third grade. A sympathetic teacher works with him, and he realizes that he can indeed do the work. He does so well that he is allowed to rejoin his classmates in fourth grade by the end of Thanksgiving. He is really happy but not prepared for what happens. As he desperately tries to fit in with the other kids, he finds himself the target of a group of bullies. The bullies get Joshua in trouble at school. Will Joshua be able to rise above the mischief or will he find himself falling back on his old behavior—the behavior that kept him back in third grade? To find out what becomes of Joshua, read Susan Shreve's *Joshua T. Bates in Trouble Again*.

Book List (Grades K–3)

Bottner, Barbara. *Bootsie Barker Bites.* Putnum & Grosset Group, 1997. (IL K–3, RL 2.8) Bootsie Barker only wants to play games in which she bites, until one day her friend comes up with a better game.

Caple, Kathy. *The Wimp.* Houghton Mifflin, 2000. (IL K–3, RL 2.5) Arnold the pig and his sister Rose give two bullying classmates a taste of their own medicine when Arnold decides he doesn't have to be a wimp anymore.

Howe, James. *Pinky and Rex and the Bully.* Atheneum Books for Young Readers, 1996. (IL K–3, RL 3.9)Pinky learns the importance of identity as he defends his favorite color, pink, and his friendship with a girl, Rex, against the neighborhood bully.

Keats, Ezra Jack. *Goggles!* Viking, 1998. (IL K–3, RL 3.1) Two boys must outsmart the neighborhood bullies before they can enjoy their new treasure, a pair of lens-less motorcycle goggles.

Kessler, Leonard P. *Last One In Is a Rotten Egg.* HarperCollins, 1999. (IL K–3, RL 1.8) After Freddy is pushed into deep water by a couple of toughs, he decides to learn to swim.

Meddaugh, Susan. *Martha Walks the Dog.* Houghton Mifflin, 1998. (IL K–3, RL 3.5) Martha the talking dog rescues the neighborhood from a bully dog with the help of a parrot.

Nickle, John. *The Ant Bully.* Scholastic Press, 1999. (IL K–3, RL 3.9) Lucas learns a lesson about bullying when he is pulled into the ant hole where he has been tormenting ants.

Pilkey, Dav. *Ricky Ricotta's Giant Robot: An Adventure Novel.* Scholastic, 2000. (IL K–3, RL 3.0) Ricky Ricotta, a small mouse, saves a giant robot from his evil creator, Dr. Stinky. In turn, the robot protects Ricky from the bullies at school and saves the city from Dr. Stinky's plan to destroy it.

Rosenberg, Liz. *Monster Mama.* Putnam & Grosset Group, 1997. (IL K–3, RL 3.7) Patrick Edward's fierce monster mother helps him deal with some obnoxious bullies.

Simon, Francesca. *Hugo and the Bullyfrogs.* David & Charles Books for Children, 1999. (IL K–3, RL 3.0) Hugo, a little frog, discovers he has a secret weapon to help him keep the bullies away.

Book List (Grades 4–6)

Cox, Judy. *Mean, Mean Maureen Green.* Holiday House, 1999. (IL 3–6, RL 3.2) With help from Adam, a boy in her third grade class, Lilley gains enough confidence to stand up to the school bus bully, Mean Maureen Green.

Duffey, Betsy. *How To Be Cool in the Third Grade.* Puffin Books, 1995. (IL 3–6, RL 3.5) When Robbie York is marked as a target by a bully at school, he decides that the only way to survive the third grade is by being cool.

Duncan, Lois. *Wonder Kid Meets the Evil Lunch Snatcher.* Little, Brown, 1988. (IL 3–6, RL 4.7) Terrorized by an evil lunch-snatcher at his new school, Brian devises, with the help of a fellow comic book fan, a plan involving a new super-hero called Wonder Kid.

Krensky, Stephen. *Louise Takes Charge.* Dial Books for Young Readers, 1998. (IL 3–6, RL 5.2) Louise enlists the aid of everyone in her class, and together they outwit Jasper the bully.

Mead, Alice. *Junebug and the Reverend.* Farrar, Straus & Giroux, 1998. (IL 3–6, RL 4.2) Having moved out of the housing project and into a new home along with his mother and sister, ten-year-old Junebug discovers that bullies are everywhere and that the elderly can be great friends.

Moss, Marissa. *Amelia Takes Command.* Pleasant Co. Publications, 1999. (IL 3–6, RL 4.2) After successfully commanding the Discovery shuttle mission at Space Camp, Amelia returns to fifth grade, where she deals with the bully who has been making her life miserable.

Roberts, Willo Davis. *The Kidnappers: A Mystery.* Atheneum Books for Young Readers, 1998. (IL 3–6, RL 5.9) No one believes 11-year-old Joey, who has a reputation for telling tall tales, when he claims to have witnessed the kidnapping of the class bully outside their expensive New York City private school.

Sachar, Louis. *The Boy Who Lost His Face.* Knopf, 1997. (IL 3–6, RL 4.4) David receives a curse from an elderly woman whom he has helped his schoolmates to attack. He learns to regret his weakness in pandering to others for the sake of popularity. Then, new friends and a very nice girl help him to be a stronger, more assertive person.

Shreve, Susan Richards. *Joshua T. Bates Takes*

Charge. Knopf, 1997, 1993. (IL 3–6, RL 5.6) Eleven-year-old Joshua, worried about fitting in at school, feels awkward when the new student he is supposed to be helping becomes the target of the fifth grade's biggest bully.

Sonenklar, Carol. *Mighty Boy*. Orchard, 1999. (IL 3–6, RL 5.0) When he gets a chance to meet his hero, the television character Mighty Boy, Howard Weinstein discovers his own strengths that help him handle the bully in his new fourth grade class.

Activities (Grades K–3)

- Lead the class in a brainstorming session about the characteristics and expected behavior of a bully. Ask the students to brainstorm some responses they can use on a bully. What types of things should they do to protect themselves?

- No one is all good or all bad. Using a character from one of the books, have students list the good things about the character as well as the bad things.

- Have the class create a "Wanted" poster for the bully in a story, including a list of the bully's outstanding characteristics.

- Help students examine the illustrations in a bully book. How does the illustrator tell the story? Invite students to create different illustrations to tell the story.

Activities (Grades 4–6)

- Ask students to brainstorm the characteristics of a bully and the types of behavior that bullies exhibit.

- In small groups, have students create board games that reward for positive behavior and punish for bullying behavior (e.g., Hold the door open for classmate—move ahead one space; Make nasty remarks about classmate—move back two spaces).

- Instruct the class to rewrite the story from another character's perspective. An example would be to tell the story from the bully's point of view or from a friend's point of view.

- Have one student narrate the story while the others act it out.

- Create a crossword puzzle listing the characteristics of a bully. Use the Puzzlemaker.com website at *http://puzzlemaker.com*.

Community

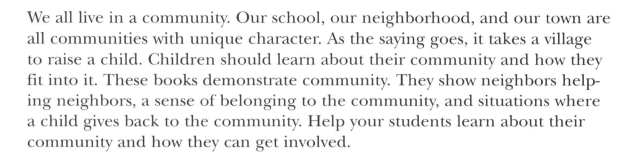

We all live in a community. Our school, our neighborhood, and our town are all communities with unique character. As the saying goes, it takes a village to raise a child. Children should learn about their community and how they fit into it. These books demonstrate community. They show neighbors helping neighbors, a sense of belonging to the community, and situations where a child gives back to the community. Help your students learn about their community and how they can get involved.

Booktalks (Grades K–3)

Momma, Where Are You From?

Bradby, Marie; ill. by Chris K. Soentpict. Orchard Books, 2000. (IL K–3, RL 3.5)

(Ask several children:) Where are you from? When someone asks you that question, you usually answer by telling where you live. In this book, when a young girl asks her mother that question, she gets a different kind of answer. Her mother tells her of the life experiences that make her the woman she is today. She is from warm summer days, from friends, family and neighbors. She lets her daughter know that you are from more than a place. So I ask you again—where are you from? To find out where Momma is from, read *Momma, Where Are You From?* by Marie Bradby.

The Summer My Father Was Ten

Brisson, Pat; ill. by Andrea Shine. Boyds Mills Press, 1998. (IL K–3, RL 5.9)

Every year my father and I plant a garden together. And every year I hear the story about the summer my father was ten. He lived with his mother in an apartment building. Mr. Bellavista lived in the same building. My father didn't know him well. He was an old man with a thick Italian accent that was hard to understand. Each summer, Mr. Bellavista cleared an abandoned lot next to the apartment building and planted a garden—that is, every summer until my father was ten. That was the year my father and his friends did something they would regret for the rest of their lives. How did it affect Mr. Bellavista? To find out, read *The Summer My Father Was Ten* by Pat Brisson.

Smoky Night

Bunting, Eve; ill. by David Diaz. Harcourt, Brace & Co., 1994. (IL K–3, RL 2.5)

Have you every heard of a riot? Maybe you've seen news reports of riots in different parts of the world. Several years ago, some of the people in Los Angeles were so angry that they started a riot. This book tells what it is like for innocent people who get caught up in the anger. A young boy and his mother stand by the window of their apartment and watch as the rioters destroy their neighborhood. The mother tries to explain the behavior to her son. Will they be safe in their apartment or will they be caught up in the insanity that has taken over? Will the neighborhood ever be the same? Read all about what happens during a *Smoky Night*.

The Piano

Miller, William; ill. by Susan Keeter. Lee & Low Books, 2000. (IL K–3, RL 4.2)

Tia loves music. While her mother is at work, Tia wanders around the neighborhood searching for the sounds of music. When she hears a song, it takes her away from the dry, dusty town she lives in and away from her poverty. She dreams of castles, mountains, and deep, new snow. On one of her wanderings, Tia finds herself on the other side of town. When she is mistakenly interviewed for a job as a cleaning lady, Tia accepts the job because she is hypnotized by the beautiful music playing in the next room. Then, Tia tries to play the piano when no one is around. What happens when Tia is discovered? Read *The Piano* by William Miller to find out.

Grandpa's Corner Store

Ryan-DiSalvo, Dyanne. HarperCollins, 2000. (IL K–3, RL 3.3)

Lucy's grandfather runs a corner grocery store in the city. Every day after school, Lucy goes to the store to wait for her mother to pick her up. Grandpa helps Lucy with her homework, and Lucy helps Grandpa with the store. Lucy loves the store, even though it is a bit run-down. But the neighborhood is changing. Old stores are being torn down and new ones are being built. When they find out that a brand new grocery store is being built just around the corner, everyone fears that it is the end of Grandpa's store. He just can't compete with a big grocery store. Lucy refuses to give up and tries everything to keep Grandpa from selling the store. Will she succeed? Does the neighborhood need to change? To find out, read *Grandpa's Corner Store* by Dyanne Ryan-DiSalvo.

Booktalks (Grades 4–6)

Lily's Crossing

Giff, Patricia Reilly. Delacorte, 1997. (IL 3–6. RL 5.2)

Lily has mixed feelings about summer vacation in 1944 during World War II. She and her grandmother will go to Rockaway as usual. Her father cannot spend the summer there, so it's just Lily and her grandmother. When they arrive at Rockaway, Lily finds out that her friend Margaret is moving away. Margaret's father has gotten a job in a factory helping with the war effort. To make matters worse, Lily's father informs her that he has enlisted and will be leaving to join the war. Lily meets a young man who is staying with neighbors and immediately decides that he is a Nazi spy. But as she gets to know Albert, she learns what a terrible price war takes on children from Europe. Spend time with Lily and Albert as they attempt to make sense of war. Learn about how a community can help people get through hard times.

When the Circus Came to Town

Horvath, Polly. Farrar, Straus & Giroux, 1996. (IL 3–6, RL 5.9)

Ten-year-old Ivy lives in a small, quiet town where not much happens—that is, until the Halibuts move in next door. You see, the Halibuts are circus people. Certainly not the kind of people the townsfolk will welcome with open arms. Then Elmira the Snake Lady moves into town. After that, the whole family of Flying Gambinis moves in. What is happening to this town? Ivy tells us how life changed in Springfield in this humorous book. Find out what happened *When the Circus Came to Town*.

The Milly Stories: Corpses, Carnations, the Wierdness Index, and, of Course, Aunt Gloria

Lindsay, Janice. DK Publishing, 1998. (IL 5–8, RL 6.2)

Aunt Gloria has died, but Milly can still hear her voice telling her to sit up straight and be a lady. Milly had come to live with Aunt Gloria and Uncle Edgar after her mother died. It was weird to be living in a funeral home, though. The other kids are wary of visiting her there. It's hard enough making friends in a new town, but this has really put a social stigma on her. And now that Aunt Gloria has died, Milly wonders what will become of her. Join Milly as she learns to listen to the voices that matter the most. To find out more about the people who live in the town, read *The Milly Stories* by Janice Lindsay.

The Muffin Child

Menick, Stephen. Philomel Books, 1998. (IL 5–8, RL 4.7)

Eleven-year-old Tanya lives on a farm in the Balkans with her parents. The year is 1913. On the way back from town, a flood collapses the bridge her parents are crossing, and they are swept out to sea. Tanya won't accept that her parents are gone forever. She refuses to stay in town with another family and insists on returning to her farm. She is desperate to have the farmhouse looking good when her parents return. She decides to make some muffins just like her mother did. These muffins turn out to be the best muffins anyone has ever tasted. Day after day, villagers come to Tanya for muffins. She starts to charge for the muffins. Soon, people from neighboring villages begin to visit to buy the wonderful muffins. As winter approaches, Tanya wonders if she can make it on her own. To find out what becomes of Tanya, read *The Muffin Child*.

Anne of Avonlea

Montgomery, Lucy Maud. Bantam Books, 1992. (IL 5–8, RL 7.8)

This is the second book in the Anne of Green Gables series. Set in Prince Edward Island in the 19th century, it continues the story of Anne Shirley. Anne is now a 16 year old who is teaching at her old school. She's also helping Marilla take care of 6-year-old twins. Anne still finds a way to mingle into others' lives and bring love and laughter to those around her. If you liked the first book, you'll enjoy this one as well. Join Anne as she continues to affect everyone in the community in *Anne of Avonlea* by Lucy Maud Montgomery.

Barber, Barbara E. *Saturday At The New You.* Lee & Low Books, 1994. (IL K–3, RL 3.1) Shauna, a young African American girl, wishes she could do more to help Momma with the customers at her beauty salon. Then one day she gets her chance.

Brisson, Pat. *Wanda's Roses.* Boyds Mills Press, 2000, 1994. (IL K–3, RL 4.3) Wanda mistakes a thorn bush for a rosebush in the empty lot. She clears away the trash around it and cares for it every day, even though no roses bloom.

DiSalvo-Ryan, DyAnne. *City Green.* Morrow Junior Books, 1994. (IL K–3, RL 3.1) Marcy and Miss Rosa start a campaign to clean up an empty lot and turn it into a community garden.

Garland, Sherry. *Summer Sands.* Harcourt Brace, 1995. (IL K–3, RL 4.8) After a winter storm destroys the sand dunes that provide a home for plants and animals, a beach community bands together to restore the dunes.

Gray, Libba Moore. *Miss Tizzy.* Simon & Schuster Books for Young Readers, 1993. (IL K–3, RL 4.2) The eccentric Miss Tizzy, a beloved friend to all the children in her neighborhood, needs their help in remaining happy when she is sick in bed.

Greenfield, Eloise. *Night On Neighborhood Street.* Puffin, 1996. (IL K–3, RL 4.7) This collection of poems explores the sounds, sights, and emotions enlivening a black neighborhood during the course of one evening.

Kalman, Bobbie. *What Is a Community? From A To Z.* Crabtree Pub., 2000. (IL K–3, RL 4.1) An alphabetical introduction to the basic concepts of community, such as buildings, family, rules, and working together.

Kurtz, Jane. *River Friendly: River Wild.* Simon & Schuster Books for Young Readers, 2000. (IL K–3, RL 2.0) Family members experience renewed appreciation for home and community after they are evacuated during a spring flood and then return to survey the damage.

Lakin, Pat. Red *Letter Day.* Raintree Steck-Vaughn, 1995. (IL K–3, RL 3.5) After visiting the local post office, Mr. Summers' third-grade class gains a greater respect for mail carriers and the work they perform.

Polacco, Patricia. *Meteor!* Putnam & Grosset Group, 1996. (IL K–3, RL 4.0) A quiet rural community is dramatically changed when a meteor crashes down in the front yard of the Gaw family.

Bonners, Susan. *Edwina Victorious.* Farrar, Straus & Giroux, 2000. (IL 3–6, RL 4.6) Edwina follows in the footsteps of her namesake great-aunt when she begins to write letters to the mayor about community problems and poses as Edwina the elder.

Dragonwagon, Crescent. *Brass Button.* Atheneum Books for Young Readers, 1997. (IL 3–6, RL 5.2) When a brass button falls off Mrs. Moffat's new coat, it begins a journey around the neighborhood and eventually ends up back where it began.

Gaeddert, LouAnn Bigge. *Hope.* Atheneum Books for Young Readers, 1995. (IL 3–6, RL 5.8) In 1851, orphans Hope and John are placed in a community of Shakers, where they encounter a way of life that is strange yet comfortable.

Lovelace, Maud Hart. *Betsy And Tacy Go Downtown.* HarperTrophy, 2000. (IL 3–6, RL 4.9) The further adventures of 12-year-old friends Betsy, Tacy, and Tib as they explore the world beyond their neighborhood and discover the public library, see a real play, and make friends with the owners of the downtown hotel.

Moses, Will. *Silent Night.* Philomel Books, 1997. (IL 3–6, RL 6.0) One snowy Christmas Eve a Vermont community makes preparations for the holiday as well as for the arrival of another Christmas miracle.

Naylor, Phyllis Reynolds. *Saving Shiloh.* Aladdin Paperbacks, 1999. (IL 3–6, RL 5.5) Sixth-grader Marty and his family try to help their rough neighbor, Judd Travers, change his mean ways, even though their West Virginia community continues to expect the worst of him.

Pellegrino, Marjorie White. *My Grandma's The Mayor.* Magination Press, 2000. (IL 3–6, RL 4.8) Annie is unhappy that she has to share her grandmother, the mayor, with so many people, but when her grandmother helps out during a town emergency, Annie appreciates all that she does in the community.

Robinson, Barbara. *The Best Christmas Pageant Ever.* HarperTrophy, 1988. (IL 3–6, RL 5.1) The six mean Herdman kids lie, steal and smoke cigars (even the girls), and then become involved in the community Christmas pageant.

Schecter, Ellen. *The Big Idea.* Hyperion Paperbacks for Children, 1996. (IL 3–6, RL 4.8) Eight-year-old Luz Mendez is determined to turn a run-down vacant lot into a garden like the one her grandmother had in Puerto Rico, but she must convince her neighbors to help.

Stuart, Jesse. *A Penny's Worth Of Character*. Jesse Stuart Foundation, 1993. (IL 3–6, RL 5.2) Shan is dishonest with the storekeeper in his rural Kentucky community, but he feels better about himself after his mother forces him to put things right.

Activities (Grades K–3)

- It is very important that students know their way around their community. Have students create a map of their neighborhood or town center. They should include landmarks such as stores, houses of people they know, and community buildings.

- A community is much more than a group of buildings. A community is people. Ask a local organization to send a representative to speak to the children about their role in the community. This could be someone from the police or fire department, a public librarian, the postmaster or postmistress, the director of parks and recreation, a newspaper editor, and so on.

- Help students research the history of their community. When was it founded? By whom? Where did it get its name? How many people live there now? What is the community well known for?

- Suggest that students write a poem about their community.

- Students can participate in a community event such as a parade, a civic ceremony or a fundraiser.

Activities (Grades 4–6)

- Most communities have areas that are in need of some extra care. Have the class adopt a spot to clean up and beautify. This can be a long-term or one-day project. Check with your community town offices to find areas appropriate for children to work on—perhaps a local park or town square. Be sure to take lots of photographs of the children working and submit a report to the local newspaper.

- Have students create an advertisement for their community. They are trying to sell their community to outsiders. They must research information and synthesize it into an advertisement. Students will work in groups.

- Encourage students to design their own community. What would it look like? What would be the unifying principle of the community? Ask them to give examples of some of the laws.

- Help students plan and carry out a community project such as a food drive, a clothing drive, or another event that can help members of the community.

- Interview someone who has lived in the community for a long time. Find out how the community has changed over the years. In their opinion, have changes been good or bad? Why?

Exceptionalities

When children encounter someone with a handicap, they often are unsure how to act. They need to be aware that people with handicaps need to be treated with respect and consideration—just as do all people. These books illustrate encounters with people with a variety of handicaps. Children will learn about the strengths and weaknesses of characters in the books. Students should be encouraged to discuss their feelings toward the characters.

Booktalks (Grades K–3)

Mama Zooms

Cowen-Fletcher, Jane. Scholastic, 1993. (IL K–3, RL 1.6)

Wow, Mama zooms! She can be anything I want her to be. She is my racehorse or my ship at sea. When I sit on my Mama's lap, we can be anything or go anywhere. You see, my Mama uses a wheelchair to get around. I love to climb into her lap and play. We play using our imagination. Sometimes, Mama is just Mama. If you want to find out the types of games we play, read *Mama Zooms.*

Be Good to Eddie Lee

Fleming, Virginia M.; ill. by Floyd Cooper. Philomel, 1993. (IL K–3, RL 4.2)

Christy's mother is always telling her to be good to Eddie Lee. He has Down's syndrome and needs a bit of kindness. Christy understands what her mother is saying, but Eddie Lee is just such a pest. She will do whatever she can to avoid him. Christy would rather spend the beautiful summer day with her friend JimBud. They are going off to explore the woods. Christy can't believe it when she finds out the Eddie Lee has followed them into the woods. JimBud tries to shoo him away, but Eddie Lee wants to stay. What Christy learns that day is how special Eddie Lee really is. He shows her a place in the woods that she had never seen. He teaches her to catch salamanders. What she learns that day changes her forever. What will you learn about Eddie Lee? Will it change you? This book will encourage you to *Be Good to Eddie Lee.*

Dad and Me in the Morning

Lakin, Patricia; ill. by Robert Steele. A. Whitman, 1994. (IL K–3, RL 2.1)

A young boy wakes up to his special alarm clock. He puts on his hearing aid and goes to wake up his father. They have a special morning ritual. They walk along the beach and observe the beauty of nature. They share the movements of the animals and the plants. Although the young boy is deaf, he and his father find many ways to communicate with each other. How many ways can you find to communicate with another person? To find out how this father and son talk to each other, read *Dad and Me in the Morning* by Patricia Lakin.

Moses Goes to School

Millman, Isaac. Farrar, Straus & Giroux, 2000. (IL K–3, RL 3.2)

Moses is excited about the first day of school. Moses goes to a special kind of school. Because he is deaf, he goes to a school for children who are deaf or hard of hearing. The children use American Sign Language, or ASL, to communicate. ASL is different from everyday English, and the children also must learn to translate ASL into English so they can communicate with others. Throughout the book, the author teaches us different signs that the children use. Join Moses and his friends as *Moses Goes to School*.

Sarah's Sleepover

Rodriguez, Bobbie; ill. by Mark Graham. Viking, 2000. (IL K–3, RL 2.7)

Sarah is so excited. She has been waiting for this weekend. It's sleepover weekend!—the weekend when her cousins are coming to the farm to visit. When the girls arrive, they all head up to Sarah's room to play. Their parents are going out and the girls are finally allowed to stay home alone. They are having a great time until a huge storm plunges their world into darkness. They are all scared—except Sarah. Sarah has been blind since birth, so she doesn't understand why the girls are so frightened by the dark. Can Sarah use her skills to calm the girls and get help? To find out, read *Sarah's Sleepover* by Bobbie Rodriguez.

Booktalks (Grades 4–6)

Joey Pigza Swallowed the Key

Gantos, Jack. Farrar, Straus & Giroux, 1998. (IL 5–8, RL 5.2)

Joey is wound up like a top. He doesn't mean to do the things he does, but he just can't help it. He just has to move. He may spin around until he falls over or runs and runs. His teachers like Joey but can't put up with his impulsive behavior. Joey is put on medication which helps calm him down, but it tends to wear off after lunch, and then Joey is moving again. Joey knows he's a disappointment to his mother and his teachers, but he just can't control himself. He's been warned that if there is one more problem, he will be sent to a special school. That one last time comes when Joey accidentally hurts another child. Find out what happens to Joey by reading *Joey Pigza Swallowed the Key*.

My Louisiana Sky

Holt, Kimberly Willis. Holt, 1998. (IL 5–8, RL 5.9)

Tiger Ann Parker is a happy little girl growing up with her parents and grandmother in Louisiana in the 1950s. She's very bright, always gets straight A's, and has won the spelling bee several years in a row. What is unusual is that both of her parents are mentally challenged. Tiger loves her parents very much despite their handicaps. It's not until she enters middle school that Tiger feels embarrassed about her parents. Kids start teasing her and she is left out. When Tiger's grandmother dies, Tiger goes to live in the city with her aunt, since her parents can't care for her on their own. At first, it's exciting to be able to reinvent herself. She cuts her hair and starts using the name Ann. The more she reinvents herself, the more Tiger comes to realize the struggles that her parents endure every day. Join Tiger on her journey of self-discovery and spend time under *My Louisiana Sky*.

Small Steps: The Year I Got Polio
Kehret, Peg. Albert Whitman & Co., 1998. (IL 3–6, RL 5.6)

Peg couldn't wait until the end of the school day. This was homecoming day, and the seventh grade float was sure to win first place. During chorus, Peg's leg kept twitching and she couldn't seem to get it to stop. On her way out of class, her leg gave out and she went down. Her books flew all over the place. When Peg went home for lunch, her mother said Peg felt hot and took her temperature. The doctor was called, and Peg knew there was no use begging to go to homecoming. As a matter of fact, all she could think about doing was sleeping. The doctor came again the next day. After examining her, he told her parents to get her to the hospital. At the hospital, they learned that she had polio. Peg had certainly heard of the illness but never knew anyone who had it. Days and nights began to blur together as Peg was transferred to another hospital. Within days, she was completely paralyzed. This is the story of the author's battle with polio. Before 1954, there was no immunization against polio. It was every parent's fear. Find out about this disease in *Small Steps: The Year I Got Polio* by Peg Kehret.

Making Room for Uncle Joe
Litchfield, Ada Bassett. Albert Whitman, 1984. (IL 3–6, RL 4.0)

When Dan learns that Uncle Joe, who has Down's syndrome, is coming to live with them, he is worried. The state home is closing, and Uncle Joe needs a place to stay until a new home can be found. Dan's friend, Ben, says he saw a television show about people with Down's syndrome and that they are all mentally retarded and look funny. Dan's sister, Beth, refuses to tell her friends about her uncle and decides that she won't invite anyone over ever again. When Uncle Joe arrives, he is friendly with the family, but Dan and Beth won't have anything to do with him. Their little sister, Amy, spends time with Uncle Joe and comes to love him. Will Dan and Beth be able to overcome their prejudice and come to love him as well? How will their friends react to Uncle Joe? Will they find a way to allow Uncle Joe to stay? Find out in *Making Room for Uncle Joe* by Ada Bassett Litchfield.

Mine for Keeps
Little, Jean. Viking, 1994. (IL 3–6, RL 4.3)

Sal has lived away from home for several years while she was learning special skills needed for a girl with cerebral palsy to get around on braces. Coming back home is full of scary surprises. With the help of Sam the dog, Sal gains enough self-confidence to open up somewhat to Piert—the new kid in town who hasn't adjusted to life in the United States. To find out what awaits Sal when she returns home, read *Mine for Keeps* by Jean Little.

Book List (Grades K–3)

Booth, Barbara D. *Mandy*. Lothrop, Lee & Shepard, 1991. (IL K–3, RL 4.8) Hearing-impaired Mandy risks going out into the scary night, during an impending storm, to look for her beloved grandmother's lost pin.

Carlson, Nancy L. *Arnie and the New Kid*. Puffin, 1992, 1990. (IL K–3, RL 1.9) When an accident requires Arnie to use crutches, he begins to understand the limits and possibilities of his new classmate, who has a wheelchair.

Condra, Estelle. *See the Ocean*. Ideals Children's Books, 1994. (IL K–3, RL 4.6) Driving through mountain fog to the beach, two young brothers compete to see who will catch the first glimpse of the ocean, but it is their blind sister Nellie who senses it first.

Davis, Patricia Anne. *Brian's Bird*. A. Whitman, 2000. (IL K–3, RL 3.0) Eight-year-old Brian, who is blind, learns how to take care of his new parakeet and comes to realize that his older brother, while sometimes careless, is not so bad after all.

Keats, Ezra Jack. *Apt. 3*. Viking, 1999. (IL K–3, RL 2.8) On a rainy day, two brothers try to discover who is playing the harmonica they hear in their apartment building.

Martin, Bill. *Knots on a Counting Rope*. Holt, 1997. (IL K–3, RL 2.8) A grandfather and his blind grandson, Boy-Strength-of-Blue-Horses, reminisce about the young boy's birth, his first horse, and an exciting horse race.

Millman, Isaac. *Moses Goes to a Concert*. Frances Foster Books, 1998. (IL K–3, RL 2.2) Moses and his schoolmates, all deaf, attend a concert where the orchestra's percussionist is also deaf. Includes illustrations in sign language and a page showing the manual alphabet.

Osofsky, Audrey. *My Buddy*. Holt, 1992. (IL K–3, RL 3.5) A young boy with muscular dystrophy tells how he is teamed up with a dog trained to do things for him that he can't do for himself.

Strom, Maria Diaz. *Rainbow Joe and Me*. Lee & Low Books, 1999. (IL K–3, RL 3.0) Eloise shares her love of colors with her blind friend Rainbow Joe, who makes his own colors when he plays beautiful notes on his saxophone.

Thompson, Mary. *My Brother, Matthew*. Woodbine House, 1992. (IL K–3, RL 4.4) Though David knows frustration and resentment at times, he feels he understands his disabled little brother even better than his parents, and together the two boys experience a great deal of joy.

Book List (Grades 4–6)

Byars, Betsy Cromer. *The Summer of the Swans*. Viking, 1970. (IL 3–6, RL 5.0) A teenage girl gains new insight into herself and her family when her cognitively challenged brother gets lost.

DeFelice, Cynthia C. *The Light on Hogback Hill*. Macmillan, 1993. (IL 3–6, RL 5.4) When she investigates the mysterious light up on Hogback Hill, 11-year-old Hadley finds and befriends a hunchbacked old woman with a tragic past.

Dorris, Michael. *Sees Behind Trees*. Hyperion Paperbacks for Children, 1997. (IL 3–6, RL 5.9) A Native American boy with a special gift to "see" beyond his poor eyesight journeys with an old warrior to a land of mystery and beauty.

Dowell, Frances O'Roark. *Dovey Coe*. Atheneum Books for Young Readers, 2000. (IL 3–6, RL 6.0) Accused of murder in her North Carolina mountain town in 1928, Dovey Coe, a strong-willed 12-year-old girl, comes to a new understanding of others, including her deaf brother, as she attempts to clear her name.

Gleitzman, Morris. *Blabber Mouth*. Harcourt Brace, 1995. (IL 3–6, RL 4.7) An Australian schoolgirl who is unable to speak is embarrassed by her father's outlandish dress and behavior.

Kurtz, Jane. *The Storyteller's Beads*. Harcourt Brace, 1998. (IL 3–6, RL 5.9) During the political strife and famine of Ethiopia in the 1980s, two Ethiopian girls, one Christian and the other Jewish and blind, struggle to overcome many difficulties, including their prejudices about each other, as they make the dangerous journey out of Ethiopia.

Robinet, Harriette. *Forty Acres and Maybe a Mule*. Aladdin Paperbacks, 2000. (IL 3–6, RL 7.1) Born with a withered leg and hand, Pascal, who is about 12 years old, joins other former slaves in a search for a farm and the freedom it promises.

Senisi, Ellen B. *Just Kids: Visiting a Class for Children with Special Needs*. Dutton Children's Books, 1998. (IL 3–6, RL 3.5) Second-grader Cindy is assigned to spend part of each day in the class for students with special needs, where she finds out that even though some kids may learn differently or have different abilities, they are all "just kids."

Taylor, Theodore. *Tuck Triumphant*. Avon, 1992. (IL 3–6, RL 6.2) Fourteen-year-old Helen, her blind dog Friar Tuck, and her family face some dramatic challenges when they discover that the Korean boy they have adopted is deaf.

Wallace, Bill. *True Friends*. Holiday House, 1994. (IL 3–6, RL 4.9) The new girl in Courtney's sixth-grade class shows her a way to survive when things at school and home begin to fall apart.

Activities (Grades K–3)

- Help students brainstorm some of the things that someone with a handicap may face. How can they help?

- Have students "interview" a character from one of the books. Students should work in groups of three or four. All students should help prepare the questions. When sharing with the class, one student should portray the interviewee and the others should take turns asking the questions.

- Handicapped people are often the victims of misunderstanding. People don't understand the strengths of the person, so they only look at the disability. Misunderstandings happen for a lot of reasons. Have the students play a game of gossip to see how a sentence can be changed just by being repeated and misunderstood.

- Have students use their other senses to gather information. They can do a blind taste test and try to identify different foods, such as salt and sugar. They can be blindfolded and given directions around obstacles. They can listen to different sounds and try to identify them.

- Invite a local expert to come in and teach the students American Sign Language. Students should learn to introduce themselves and communicate simple phrases such as "hello" and "goodbye."

Activities (Grades 4–6)

- Assign students to work in groups researching a particular disability. They should prepare a booklet with important information about the disability. This can be shared with the class.

- Have students write a "five senses poem." The poem should describe an object:

  It smells like...
  It tastes like...
  It looks like...
  It sounds like...
  It feels like...

- Write a letter to the author of the book. The students should tell what they learned by reading the book and what it meant to them. They should note whether they have had contact with a disabled person.

- Begin a study of the Braille alphabet, its origins and how it is used. Then have students write their name in Braille.

- Help students experience what it is like to have a disability for a day. Have them attempt to do their everyday tasks in the library or classroom, and supply them with props to achieve their disability status. After the experience, have students write a journal entry explaining what they experienced and what emotions they went through.

Exploring Friendships

Having friends is important to each of us. Many of us have one or two "best" friends with whom we spend lots of time. Sometimes our friends are people we only see in specific situations like sports or clubs. Sometimes it is difficult to make friends. Sometimes being a friend can be difficult too. This unit covers books that discuss friends and friendships.

Booktalks (Grades K–3)

Best Friends

Cohen, Miriam; ill. by Lillian Hoban. MacMillan Publishing, 1971. (IL K–3, RL 2.6)

Do you have a best friend? Not just a friend, but a really best friend? Have you ever had a fight with your best friend over something that wasn't your fault? That's what happens to Jim. His best friend is Paul, but as the day goes on and more and more things go wrong, Paul begins to doubt that Jim feels that they are best friends. Can they figure out what is going on and go back to being best friends? Read *Best Friends* to find out.

Best Friends for Frances

Hoban, Russell; ill. by Lillian Hoban. Harper Row, 1969. (IL K–3, RL 3.5)

Have you ever gone over to someone's house to play but they don't want to? Frances wants to play ball with her friend Albert. He can't, though. Today is his wandering day, and he wants to be alone. He can't play the next day, either, because he's involved in a no-girls baseball game. Frances is left with Gloria—her too-young sister who can't do much. As Frances plays with Gloria, she comes to understand that a sister can also be a friend. Together, they teach Albert what it is to be a best friend.

Horace and Morris but Mostly Dolores

Howe, James; ill. by Amy Walrod. Atheneum Books for Young Readers, 1999. (IL K–3, RL 2.0)

Horace, Morris and Dolores do everything together. They are the best of friends. They know they will always be best friends—that is, until the day Horace and Morris join a "boys only" club. Dolores is not welcome. Dolores decides to form her own club—a "girls only" club. Even though they each have new friends and enjoy being with them, they miss their old friendships as well. Is it too late to be friends again? To find out, read *Horace and Morris but Mostly Dolores* by James Howe.

Best Friends

Kellogg, Steven. Dial Books for Young Readers, 1986. (IL K–3, RL 3.9)

Do you have a best friend with whom you share everything? Kathy does. Her best friend is Louise Jenkins, and they do everything together. They share their chocolate milk and ride their imaginary pony. Then something terrible happens. Louise's aunt and uncle take her camping for the summer. Kathy can't believe it. A whole summer without Louise is unbearable. She is so lonely and believes that Louise is lonely too. When she finds out that Louise is having a great time and making new friends, Kathy gets really angry. She decides that Louise was her very worst friend—not her best friend. Will the girls get over this when Louise returns? To find out, read *Best Friends* by Steven Kellogg.

Best Friends Sleep Over.

Rogers, Jacqueline. Scholastic, 1993. (IL K–3, RL 2.5)

Have you ever gone to a sleepover at a friend's house? Well, Gilbert hasn't! He is about to go on his very first sleepover. He is really nervous. What if he can't find the bathroom in the night? What if he can't fall asleep? His mother tries to reassure him that everything will be fine, but Gilbert isn't too sure. The evening goes great. The boys have fun playing together. But when it's time for bed, Gilbert gets really homesick and starts to cry. Will he be able to spend the whole night, or will he call his mother to pick him up? Can his friends convince him to stay? Find out in *Best Friends Sleep Over* by Jacqueline Rogers.

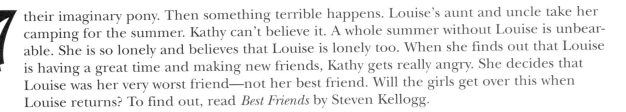

Booktalks (Grades 4–6)

On My Honor

Bauer, Marion Dane. Clarion, 1986. (IL 5–8, RL 5.6)

Have you ever had a best friend who was so different from you that you couldn't understand why you were friends? Joel Bates and Tony Zabrinsky are very different, but they've been friends all their lives. Tony tends to be a bit reckless and daring. When he suggests they climb the bluffs at Starved Rock Park, Joel doesn't want to go but doesn't want to admit he's afraid. Along the way, Joel and Tony exchange dares and insults. When Joel dares Tony to swim out to the sandbar, he doesn't know that Tony can't swim. Tony tries anyway. To find out what happens, read *On My Honor* by Marion Dane Bauer.

The Frog Princess of Pelham

Conford, Ellen. Little, Brown, 1997. (IL 5–8, RL 4.1)

Chandler had everything that money could buy. She had everything except love. Orphaned at age nine, Chandler lived with her cousin, Horace, who was more interested in spending her money than caring for her. Chandler was not looking forward to school vacation week. Horace was off to Switzerland, and he had arranged for Chandler to spend the week at a survival camp in the mountains. Chandler had few friends in school. She was far from popular—especially with the boys. She thought it was a dream when Danny Malone asked her for a kiss. And what a kiss it was! Chandler felt she was melting. When she opened her eyes, the world looked so different. All she could see was Danny's foot. He looked like a giant. And she suddenly had a craving for flies. Is it possible that she had turned into a frog? If so, how could she get back to her old self? How can her new friends help her? Read *The Frog Princess of Pelham* by Ellen Conford to find out.

Meet Calliope Day

Haddad, Charles. Delacorte, 1998. (IL 3–6, RL 5.2)

Sometimes you just can't predict who will end up becoming friends. Take, for instance, Calliope Day. Calliope is a young girl who falls into unexpected and bizarre adventures. Funny and endearing, Calliope believes that her neighbor, Mrs. Blatherhorn, is a witch.

She decides to make friends with Mrs. B. to learn all about her. What she finds may surprise you. Read *Meet Calliope Day* to find out all about Mrs. B.

When Zachary Beaver Came to Town

Holt, Kimberly Willis. Holt, 1999. (IL 5–8, RL 5.0)

Have you ever met someone who is really different from anyone else you've ever met? How did you react? Do you just avoid the person? Or were you curious about this strange person? Well, in this book, you'll find plenty of strange characters. First you'll meet Toby. Then you'll meet his dad—a postman who raises worms. You'll meet his mom, who wants to be a country and western singer. His best friend is Cal, who has a brother serving in Vietnam. Cal tends to be a bit crazy. But the oddest character of all is Zachary Beaver. Zachary Beaver is a 600-pound boy who lives in a trailer. With all these characters around, it's not hard to wonder who will be friends with Toby.

Losers, Inc.

Mills, Claudia. Farrar, Straus & Giroux, 1997. (IL 5–8, RL 4.2)

Ethan Winfield and Julius Zimmerman think of themselves as sixth grade losers. They aren't good students. They aren't good athletes. Just about everything they do is doomed to failure. Even their names put them at the end of the alphabet. Things change for Ethan when Ms. Gunderson begins her student teaching in his science class. She's beautiful and seems to think Ethan has more to offer than he's been showing. Ethan decides to work as hard as he can to impress his student teacher. Will he risk losing his best friend in the process? Follow Ethan as he finds that you don't always have to be a loser.

Brett, Jan. *Annie and the Wild Animals*. Houghton Mifflin, 1985. (IL K–3, RL 2.5) When Annie's cat disappears, she attempts friendship with a variety of unsuitable woodland animals, but with the emergence of spring, everything improves.

Cohen, Miriam. *Will I Have a Friend?* Aladdin Books, 1986. (IL K–3, RL 2.6) Jim's anxieties on his first day of school are happily forgotten when he makes a new friend.

Giff, Patricia Reilly. *Good Luck, Ronald Morgan!* Viking, 1996. (IL K–3, RL 2.2) Ronald Morgan needs lots of luck to train the dog he just received for his birthday and win the friendship of his new neighbor.

Heine, Helme. *Friends*. Aladdin Books, 1986. (IL K–3, RL 3.5) Three friends who love to be together come to the realization that sometimes it's just not possible to be together.

Henkes, Kevin. *Chester's Way*. Mulberry Books, 1997. (IL K–3, RL 3.1) Chester and Wilson share the same way of doing things, until Lilly moves into the neighborhood and shows them that new ways can be just as good.

Henkes, Kevin. *Jessica*. Mulberry Books, 1998. (IL K–3, RL 1.9) Ruthie does everything with her imaginary friend Jessica. Then, on her first day at kindergarten, she meets a real new friend with the same name.

Hutchins, Pat. *My Best Friend*. Greenwillow Books, 1993. (IL K–3, RL 1.6) Despite differences in abilities, two little girls appreciate each other and are best friends.

Lobel, Arnold. *Frog and Toad Are Friends*. HarperCollins Publishers, 1970. (IL K–3, RL 2.4) Five tales recounting the adventures of two best friends—Frog and Toad.

Monson, A. M. *Wanted—Best Friend*. Dial Books for Young Readers, 1997. (IL K–3, RL 2.8) Cat advertises for a new playmate when his best friend Mouse refuses to play checkers.

Steig, William. *Amos & Boris*. Farrar, Straus & Giroux, 1971. (IL K–3, RL 3.7) Befriended by a whale as he is drowning in the ocean, a mouse gets a chance to reciprocate years later in an equally unlikely situation.

Baker, Barbara. *The William Problem*. Puffin Books, 1997. (IL 3–6, RL 3.5) Liza hates third grade because she is separated from her best friend and she has mean Mrs. Rumford as her teacher. Then she begins to make new friends.

Carbone, Elisa Lynn. *Sarah and the Naked Truth*. Alfred A. Knopf; distributed by Random House, 2000. (IL 5–8, RL 5.4) While ten-year-old Sarah faces some challenges after losing most of her hair in a bubble gum accident, her closest friends Christina and Olivia deal with identity issues of their own, and in the end all learn to stand up to others in order to be true to themselves.

Carbone, Elisa Lynn. *Starting School with an Enemy*. Alfred A. Knopf; distributed by Random House, 1998. (IL 3–6, RL 6.1) Worried about finding friends when she moves from Maine to Maryland, ten-year-old Sarah gets off to a bad start by making an enemy of a boy.

Franklin, Kristine L. *Lone Wolf*. Candlewick Press, 1998. (IL 5–8, RL 4.8) When a large family moves into the house near where Perry and his father live in the woods, Perry's friendship with the oldest girl helps him come to terms with his sister's death and his parents' divorce.

Johnson, Angela. *Maniac Monkeys on Magnolia Street*. Alfred A. Knopf; distributed by Random House, 1999. (IL 3–6, RL 4.8) Ten-year-old Charlie adjusts to her move to a new neighborhood when she befriends Billy, with whom she hunts maniac monkeys, braves Mr. Pinkbelly's attack cat, and digs for fossils and treasure.

Kehret, Peg. *The Richest Kids in Town*. Pocket, 1997. (IL 3–6, RL 4.2) New to town and homesick for his old life, Peter Dodge teams up with a classmate to earn money for a trip to visit his best friend, but all their moneymaking schemes have unexpected results.

Levine, Gail Carson. *The Wish*. HarperCollins, 2000. (IL 5–8, RL 4.8) When granted her wish to be the most popular girl in school, Wilma, an eighth grader, forgets that she will graduate in three weeks and her popularity will vanish.

Levy, Elizabeth. *Seventh-Grade Tango*. Hyperion Books for Children, 2000. (IL 5–8, RL 5.8) When Rebecca, a seventh-grader, is paired up with her friend Scott for a dance class at school, she learns a lot about who her real friends are.

Spinelli, Jerry. *Crash*. Alfred A. Knopf, 1996. (IL 3–6, RL 4.8) Seventh-grader John "Crash" Coogan has always been comfortable with his tough, aggressive behavior, until his relationship with an unusual Quaker boy and his grandfather's stroke make him consider the meaning of friendship and the importance of family.

Ware, Cheryl. *Flea Circus Summer*. Orchard Books, 1997. (IL 3–6, RL 4.8) The summer before seventh grade, Venola Mae Cutright, the best newspaper carrier in Belington, West Virginia, writes a series of humorous letters to her best friend away at camp, the Ultra Underwater Flea Circus Company, and her newspaper boss.

Activities (Grades K–3)

- Have students draw self-portraits. Display the portraits on the wall to create a friendship mural.

- Family members can be friends also. Ask students to describe who is their best family friend and why.

- Host a friendship snack time. Students can bring in snacks to share with others.

- Brainstorm the qualities of a friend. What do you look for in a friend? What makes a good friend? Keep a chart of ideas on the wall. Add new qualities as the children read their books and gain insight into the concept of friendship.

- Direct students in an activity designed to help them get to know other students better. As students enter the room, give each one half of a paper heart with a jagged edge. Explain that they must search for the student with other half of their heart paper, then spend the day as best friends might.

Activities (Grades 4–6)

The following activities can enhance students' exploration of the concept of friendship.

- Brainstorm the qualities of a friend. What do you look for in a friend? What makes a good friend? Keep a chart of ideas on the wall. Add new qualities as the children read their books and gain insight into the concept of friendship.

- Pair students to improvise and share scenes to illustrate the concept of friendship. Students can be given a scenario to act out and then illustrate how they would expect a friend to behave in that circumstance.

- Have students draw the name of another student out of a hat for a "secret friend." The students will try to do something good for their "secret friend" throughout the day. This activity can be repeated daily or weekly if desired. Reveal the secret friends at the end of the day and have students discuss just what was done during the day to make them feel as if they had a friend.

- Have students create a "Me Museum" by filling a paper bag with items from home that tell others who they are. Items can include vacation souvenirs, family photos, and prizes.

- Using pictures with blank conversation bubbles, ask students to fill in the dialog based on their understanding of what is being portrayed in the picture.

Family

Families come in all shapes and sizes. Some function better than others, but no one definition of what makes a family is better than another. No matter what the family is like, chances are it is the most influential group of people in a child's life. Families impart values—both good and bad. Families are role models of acceptable behavior. These books all show family situations that children may encounter. These should lead to some interesting discussions.

Booktalks (Grades K–3)

My Family Vacation

Khalsa, Dayal Kaur. Clarkson N. Potter, 1988. (IL K–3, RL 3.1)

Have you ever gone on a family vacation? Don't you just love seeing new places and doing new things? Well, May has never been on a family vacation. She is excited and helps her dad pack up the car. They are driving all the way to Florida for a vacation. Just as they are about to leave, it starts to snow. May is sad to leave the snow, but her parents tell her that she'll soon forget all about that. May and her family stay in different hotels on their way to Florida, and May collects souvenirs at each stop. Join May and her family on *My Family Vacation* by Dayal Kaur Khalsa.

Daughter's Day Blues

Pegram, Laura; ill. by Cornelius Van Wright and Ying-Hwa Hu. Dial Books for Young Readers, 2000. (IL K–3, RL 3.6)

Do you have a little brother who seems to mess up everything? Well, Phyllis Mae sure does. Phyllis Mae has spent a lot of time helping make a cake for Mother's Day. But her little brother J. T. knocks it on the floor and ruins everything. It seems as if J. T. ruins everything that is important to Phyllis Mae. Nana comes up with an idea to celebrate Daughter's Day, and Momma will get time off from work to come to the party. All week long, Phyllis and Nana work on getting ready for the party. All week long, J. T. ruins the plans. He knocks over the cups and he lets the balloons fly away. Will they ever be able to pull off a Daughter's Day party without J. T. ruining it? To find out, read *Daughter's Day Blues*.

Trade-In Mother

Russo, Marisabina. Greenwillow Books, 1993. (IL K–3, RL 2.3)

Max has had it with his mother! Has your mother ever done things that make you mad? Max's mother sure has today. She forgot to buy his favorite cereal, so he had to have something different for breakfast. She made him wear a coat to school even though he said he didn't need one. She dragged him along to his sister's Girl Scout meeting. Max decides he will trade his mother in. His mother asks him what kind of mother he wants to trade her for. To find out, read *Trade-in Mother* by Marisabina Russo.

Jonathan and His Mommy

Smalls-Hector, Irene; ill. by Michael Hays. Little, Brown, 1992. (IL K–3, RL 1.9)

Do you have a special routine you do with a parent or friend? Maybe you have a special phrase you say at certain times. Maybe you have a special chant while riding in the car, or a certain song to sing at bedtime. These are some of your family traditions. Jonathan and his mother have their own special tradition. It involves their daily walk. They don't just walk around the neighborhood. They giant step, reggae step, running step and a lot more. Join the fun in *Jonathan and His Mommy*.

Grandad Bill's Song

Yolen, Jane; ill. by Melissa Bay Mathis. Philomel Books, 1994. (IL K–3, RL 2.5)

It's wonderful to have family around, but sometimes people we love pass away. It is very hard to understand what is happening. In this book, a young boy is trying to come to terms with the death of his grandfather. He asks a variety of people what they did the day Grandad Bill died. They all try to explain how they felt and what they did. Can the young boy come to understand his own feelings? Read *Grandad Bill's Song* to find out.

Booktalks (Grades 4–6)

The Many Troubles of Andy Russell

Alder, David. Harcourt Brace, 1998. (IL 3–6, RL 4.2)

Andy isn't sure he is ready for his parents to have another baby. He is sure his best friend needs a home. Tamika's parents have been hurt in a car accident and can't take care of Tamika. Andy decides that his parents should help, and he starts proceedings to have Tamika placed in his home with his family. Find out what happens in *The Many Troubles of Andy Russell*.

Getting Near to Baby

Couloumbis, Audrey. Putnam, 1999. (IL 5–8, RL 5.0)

My life has changed so much and I don't really like it. I want to be back in my own room with my mother and my sisters. It's been a while since Little Sister and I came to live with Aunt Patty and Uncle Hob. They mean well, but they've never had any kids of their own. They can't understand what we are doing. Aunt Patty just wants to dress us up like dolls and parade us around town. She invites the most obnoxious girl over to play with us just because Aunt Patty wants to get into some social circle. And worse yet, she wants to do something drastic to Little Sister just to get her to start talking again. Can't she just understand that Little Sister will talk when she has something to say? And Mom. She just needs her time too. We all do. So, Little Sister and I will sit out here on the roof of Aunt Patty's house until we feel we have had enough time. Join Little Sister and me as we are *Getting Near to Baby*.

Freaky Friday

Rodgers, Mary. Harper, 1972. (IL 5–8, RL 6.0)

Have you ever wished that you could change places with someone for just one day? Annabel Andrews does. She is tired of all her mother's rules. She doesn't understand why her mother won't let her live on marshmallows and stay out with her friends. When Annabel wakes up in her mother's body, she is amazed. She wants to make the most of it and pretends to be her mother. She tries to take care of the laundry and the cooking but

finds out things are harder than they look. When she meets with Annabel's teachers, she is amazed that they really do care about her and want her to live up to her potential. Annabel (as her mother) vows to the teachers that Annabel will turn herself around. Annabel wonders what her mother has been doing all day as Annabel. Find out how this tale ends. Read *Freaky Friday* by Mary Rodgers.

101 Ways To Bug Your Parents
Wardlaw, Lee. Yearling Books, 1998. (IL 3–6, RL 4.8)

How many ways can you think of to bug your parents? I'm sure there are lots. Sneeze Wyatt has come up with at least 101. When his parents force him to take a summer school course in writing, he has more reason to want to bug his parents. All the children in the summer school class are expected to write a book. The other kids talk Sneeze into putting his 101 ways into a book even though the teacher has reservations about this endeavor. As his classmates start asking to buy copies of the book, Sneeze sees a great way to earn enough money to attend the Invention Convention that his parents won't let him go to. How many of these *101 Ways to Bug Your Parents* have you tried?

Out of the Storm
Willis, Patricia. Avon, 1995. (IL 3–6, RL 4.2)

Mandy's life has changed forever, and she's not happy about it. Her father has died during World War II, and she and her mother have moved to Aunt Bess' farm. Life on the farm is very different from what Mandy is used to. Mandy must tend to the sheep but dreams of the time when they will have enough money to go home. Mandy's mother has other ideas, though. She has decided to buy a small store and start life again. This is just not acceptable to Mandy, and she does all she can to sabotage the sale. Will Mandy stop living in the past and be able to find the good in her new life? Read *Out of the Storm* to find out.

Book List (Grades K–3)

Baker, Barbara. *One Saturday Morning*. Puffin, 1997. (IL K–3, RL 1.7) One Saturday a family enjoys such activities as getting up one by one, going to the park, and eating spaghetti for lunch.

Heide, Florence Parry. *Sami and the Time of the Troubles*. Clarion, 1992. (IL K–3, RL 4.9) A ten-year-old Lebanese boy goes to school, helps his mother with chores, plays with his friends, and lives with his family in a basement shelter when bombings occur and fighting begins on his street.

Joosse, Barbara M. *Snow Day!* Clarion, 1995. (IL K–3, RL 2.4) When school is cancelled because of snow, Robby and his family enjoy the day together.

Kaplan, Howard. *Waiting To Sing*. DK Ink, 2000. (IL K–3, RL 3.8) A family that loves music and spends many hours at the piano is devastated by the death of the mother, but those still living find consolation in the beautiful music that also remains.

Kirk, Daniel. *Snow Family*. Hyperion Books for Children, 2000. (IL K–3, RL 3.1) A young boy decides to build a snow family to take care of his snowboy the way his parents take care of him.

McCloskey, Robert. *Make Way for Ducklings*. Puffin, 1999. (IL K–3, RL 3.1) A family of mallard ducks searches for a new home in Boston.

Ormerod, Jan. *Who's Whose?* Lothrop, Lee & Shepard, 1998. (IL K–3, RL 3.5) Three busy families engage in such activities as school, soccer, piano playing, and cooking.

Rylant, Cynthia. *The Relatives Came*. Aladdin Paperbacks, 1993, 1985. (IL K–3, RL 3.1) The relatives come to visit from Virginia, and everyone has a wonderful time.

Shelby, Anne. *Homeplace*. Orchard Books, 2000. (IL K–3, RL 3.5) A grandmother and grandchild trace their family history and the growth of their home from a log cabin to a large farmhouse.

Williams, Vera B. *A Chair for My Mother*. Mulberry, 1993. (IL K–3, RL 3.8) A child, her waitress mother, and her grandmother save dimes to buy a comfortable armchair after all their furniture is lost in a fire. Includes study guide.

Book List (Grades 4–6)

Carlson, Natalie Savage. *The Family Under the Bridge*. HarperCollins, 1986. (IL 3–6, RL 5.1) An old tramp, adopted by three fatherless children when their mother hides them under a bridge on the Seine, finds a home for mother and children and a job for himself.

Cleary, Beverly. *Ramona Quimby, Age 8*. Morrow, 1981. (IL 3–6, RL 5.3) The further adventures of the Quimby family as Ramona enters third grade.

Creech, Sharon. *The Wanderer*. HarperCollins Publishers, 2000. (IL 3–6, RL 5.7) Thirteen-year-old Sophie and her cousin Cody record their transatlantic crossing aboard the Wanderer, a 45-foot sailboat, which they and their uncles and another cousin take to visit their grandfather in England.

Curtis, Christopher Paul. *The Watsons Go to Birmingham—1963: A Novel*. Delacorte Press, 1995. ((IL 5–8, RL 5.0) The ordinary interactions and everyday routines of the Watsons, an African-American family living in Flint, Michigan, are drastically changed after they go to visit Grandma in Alabama in the summer of 1963.

Hesse, Karen. *Out of the Dust*. Scholastic, 1999. (IL 3–6, RL 4.5) In a series of poems, 15-year-old Billie Jo relates the hardships of living on her family's wheat farm in Oklahoma during the dust bowl years of the Depression.

Hest, Amy. *The Private Notebook of Katie Roberts, Age 11*. Candlewick Press, 1996. (IL 3–6, RL 4.0) In a series of journal entries and letters to a pen pal, Katie relates her feelings about her father's death in World War II, her mother's remarriage, and the family's move from New York City to Texas.

Kinsey-Warnock, Natalie. *The Canada Geese Quilt*. Cobblehill Books/Dutton, 1989. (IL 3–6, RL 4.7) Worried that the coming of a new baby and her grandmother's serious illness will change the warm, familiar life on her family's Vermont farm, 10-year-old Ariel combines her artistic talent with her grandmother's knowledge to make a very special quilt.

Mead, Alice. *Soldier Mom*. Farrar, Straus & Giroux, 1999. (IL 3–6, RL 4.0) Eleven-year-old Jasmyn gets a different perspective on life when her mother is sent to Saudi Arabia at the beginning of the Persian Gulf War, leaving her and her baby half brother behind in Maine in the care of her mother's boyfriend.

Naylor, Phyllis Reynolds. *Shiloh*. Aladdin Paperbacks, 2000. (IL 3–6, RL 5.7) When he finds a lost beagle in the hills behind his West Virginia home, Marty tries to hide it from his family and the dog's real owner, a mean-spirited man known to shoot deer out of season and to mistreat his dogs.

Raskin, Ellen. *Figgs & Phantoms*. Puffin Books, 1989. (IL 3–6, RL 5.5) Chronicles the adventures of the unusual Figg family after they left show business and settled in the town of Pineapple.

Activities (Grades K–3)

- Brainstorm "What is a family?" What defines a family? Do you need to be related by blood? Accept all answers.

- Ask students to make a list of people in their lives that they would define as family.

- Have students fill in as many answers as they can to the statement "I am like my family because _____" (e.g., same color hair, same laugh, same likes)

- Have students interview their parent(s) about what life was like when they were young. What was school like? What kinds of clothes did they wear? What games did they play? What did they do for fun? Share with the class.

- Have students make a picture book (with at least eight scenes) that describes their family.

Activities (Grades 4–6)

- Brainstorm what makes up a family. Do families need to be related by blood, or can other ties make a family?

- Have students find out about their families. Where did they come from? Have they always lived in this town? Where are relatives located?

- Survey the students to find out how many siblings they have. Using computer-graphing software, have students graph the results. What is the largest number? The smallest number? All male? All female? Twins or other multiples?

- Discuss the different roles that people play within a family. There are traditional roles such as breadwinner and homemaker. What are some other roles people play? (e.g. peacemaker, comedian, scholar)

- Have students make an accordion book about their family. Take several pieces of paper of the same size. Tape the sheets together along the edges. Fold into an accordion style. Cut yarn to wrap around the book to hold it together. You can have students organize their work independently or give them a template to work from (for instance, page one: child's name, page two: parents, page three: place of birth, page four: favorites, and so on).

Heroes

We all have our heroes and heroines. Sometimes these are deserving people; sometimes they're not. Children need to know what a hero really is. Too many children look up to sports figures and music stars and not notice local heroes in their midst such as police and firefighters. In this section, we look at books that illustrate the notion of a hero. They are not necessarily rich and famous; they may be as ordinary as a sibling or a neighbor. Their actions are what make them heroes. Children should gain an understanding of how even ordinary people can become heroes.

Booktalks (Grades K–3)

The Bravest of Us All

Arnold, Marsha Diane; ill. by Brad Sneed. Dial Books for Young Readers, 2000. (IL K–3, RL 2.7)

Do you know someone who is brave?...someone who can do brave things? Do you admire that person? Do you think that he or she is a hero? Well, in this story, Ruby Jane thinks her sister Velma Jane is the bravest person in the world. She can walk barefoot across the hot sand, break in a new colt, or cross the field with the mean old bull. Ruby Jane is afraid of everything. When a storm threatens to turn into a tornado, one of these girls will really become a hero. Can you figure out which one? To find out, read *The Bravest of Us All* by Marsha Diane Arnold.

Radio Rescue

Barasch, Lynne. Frances Foster Books, 2000. (IL K–3, RL 3.4)

Back in the 1920s, things sure were different than they are today. Communication certainly wasn't as advanced. If you wanted to make a long distance telephone call, it might take hours to be connected. You would call one operator who then called another and then another, until finally they were able to connect you. It was sort of like passing a note in class: You give it to one person who passes it to another person who passes it to another until it gets to the person who's supposed to read it. There was no way to make a telephone call overseas because there were no telephone wires in the ocean. Long before the Internet and online chat came into common practice, people found a way to communicate all around the world using a wireless radio. You couldn't speak on these but you could communicate using a sound. A code was developed that radio operators could use to understand each other. (Show the page of the book with the code.) This was called Morse code, and it took some work to learn. In this story, a young man is determined to learn the code and become a licensed radio operator. People were not allowed to transmit on the radio unless they were licensed. Once he received his license, he had a lot of fun communicating with people all around the world. He had no idea that his hobby would make him a hero. To find out what happens and what he does, read *Radio Rescue* by Lynne Barasch.

Swimmy

Lionni, Leo. Alfred A. Knopf, 1991. (IL K–3, RL 3.0)

Swimmy was a happy little fish. He loved to swim with the other fish in his school. He wasn't like the rest of the fish, though. He was a black fish. All the other fish in his school were red. One day as they were swimming, a great big fish came along and swallowed up all the fish except Swimmy. All alone and lonely, Swimmy set off to find a new school of fish to swim with. On his journey, he discovered many new things. When he finally met up with a new school of red fish, he found out that they were in trouble. Can Swimmy come up with a plan to help them? To find out, read *Swimmy* by Leo Lionni.

Pink and Say

Polacco, Patricia. Philomel Books, 1994. (IL K–3, RL 4.9)

This is the story of two teenagers—one white and one black. During the Civil War, it was not uncommon for teens to go to war. Pink, a teenage slave from the South, and Say, a white teen from Ohio, are brought together on the battlefield. They are both fighting for the Union Army. Say has been injured and left for dead. Pink has been separated from his company and is searching for them when he comes across Say. Pink just can't leave him there to die, so he risks his own life to take Say back to the plantation in enemy territory where Pink's mother can help. The plantation is in ruins, and Pink's mother, Moe Moe Bay, is the only one left. She nurses Say back to health. She is risking a great deal to help the boys, because she could be shot for helping Union soldiers. Both Pink and Moe Moe Bay risk their lives to help a poor white boy they don't even know. This book is filled with heroic deeds. Will Pink, Say and Moe Moe Bay be okay? To find out, read *Pink and Say* by Patricia Polacco.

Shy Charles

Wells, Rosemary. Dial Books for Young Readers, 1988. (IL K–3, RL 3.1)

Do you sometimes feel shy, like you just don't want to meet new people or do new things? Do you have trouble talking with people you don't know? Well, Charles certainly does. When his mother takes him shopping, he hides rather than talk with the sales lady. At dance class, he pretends to be asleep so he doesn't have to participate. When his babysitter is hurt, Charles must overcome his shyness to help her. Will he be able to help or will he hide somewhere? Will he ever overcome his shyness? Read *Shy Charles* by Rosemary Wells to find out.

Booktalks (Grades 4–6)

Tracks in the Snow

Bledsoe, Lucy Jane. Holiday House, 1997. (IL 3–6, RL 3.5)

When Erin's babysitter Amy does not show up when she's supposed to, Erin's parents are convinced that Amy is just an irresponsible teenager. Erin doesn't believe that, though. She and Amy are friends. Amy has confided in Erin about a secret cabin in the woods that she hopes to live in one day. Erin is told that Amy and her mother have moved to Tucson, but Amy certainly would have said goodbye. When Erin is assigned a science project, she decides to study animal tracks in the snow. This is a perfect excuse to go looking for Amy. Unfortunately, Erin's study partner Tiffany insists on going along. What the two girls don't know is that a storm is coming and they won't make it out of the woods that day. Just how far will Erin go to help her friend? Join Erin and Tiffany as they try to survive after following *Tracks in the Snow*.

My Dog, My Hero

Byars, Betsy Cromer. Holt, 2000. (IL 3–6, RL 5.0)

Heroes come in all shapes and sizes. They even can be man's best friend. Have you ever heard news stories about dogs saving people? There are dogs who can dial 911 in an emergency, and dogs who wake up their owners during fires to get them out safely. This is the story of eight dogs who are competing for the title of "hero of the year." There's Smiley, who fought a dangerous bull, and Buster, who pulled a baby carriage out of the way of a truck. Do you want to know more? Do you think you can guess which dog will wear the hero medal? To find out more, read *My Dog, My Hero* by Betsy Cromer Byars.

Why Not, Lafayette?

Fritz, Jean. Putnam, 1999. (IL 3–6, RL 5.0)

As a young boy in France, Gilbert Lafayette longed for glory. Born into a noble household, the young Marquis de Lafayette spent his days listening to stories of ancestors who had won glory. He even had a relative who fought under Joan of Arc. When young Lafayette heard of the revolution happening in America, he traveled across the ocean to join George Washington and the brave American soldiers. He soon found himself in command of a group of ragtag Americans with few supplies. Lafayette proved himself to be a true friend of the American cause and a great leader. To find out more about Lafayette, read *Why Not, Lafayette?* by Jean Fritz.

Julie of the Wolves

George, Jean Craighead. Harper & Row, 1973. (IL 5–8, RL 5.6)

A 15-year-old Eskimo girl has a pen pal in San Francisco. Married—and hating it—she decides to venture off from Alaska to San Francisco in search of a better life. *Julie of the Wolves* is the story of Miyak (Julie) struggling to survive in the tundra, where lichen and lemmings are a food treat. We think alongside Julie as she learns old ways and Eskimo ways to get through cold arctic trek as part of the wolf family she has adopted. To find out what happens to Julie, read *Julie of the Wolves* by Jean Craighead George.

A Boy and His Bear

Graham, Harriet. McElderry Books, 1996. (IL 3–6, RL 5.2)

This story takes place in England in medieval times, when the sport of bearbaiting is popular. Bearbaiting involves chaining a bear and forcing it to fight for its life. When young Dickon is sent to London Bear Garden on an errand, he finds a young bear cub that is being chased by the handlers. Dickon loves animals and is determined to save this young bear from a cruel future. Medieval London comes alive in this book. This book is told partly from the bear cub's point of view. To find out if Dickon will be successful in his quest to save the bear, read *A Boy and His Bear* by Harriet Graham.

Bridwell, Norman. *Clifford to the Rescue*. Scholastic, 2000. (IL K–3, RL 2.3) Clifford uses his size to help out in many ways—saving a kitten, rescuing people from a fire and supporting a bridge so a parade can pass.

Graham, Bob. *Max*. Candlewick Press, 2000. (IL K–3, RL 2.9) Max, the young son of superheroes, is a late bloomer when it comes to flying, until he is inspired by the plight of a falling baby bird.

Lakin, Pat. *Where There's Smoke*. Raintree Steck-Vaughn, 1995. (IL K–3, RL 2.5) When Karen and Melissa report a fire at the local variety store, they are invited to go to the fire station to learn how firefighters do their jobs.

Lindgren, Astrid. *Pippi to the Rescue*. Viking, 2000. (IL K–3, RL 3.1) The heroic Pippi Longstocking takes charge and rescues two little boys from a burning building when no one else can figure out how to save them.

Luenn, Nancy. *Nessa's Fish*. Aladdin Paperbacks, 1997. (IL K–3, RL 3.9) Nessa's ingenuity and bravery save from animal poachers the fish she and her grandmother caught to feed everyone in their Eskimo camp.

Mountbatten-Windsor, Sarah, Duchess of York. *Budgie at Bendick's Point*. Simon & Schuster Books for Young Readers, 1989. (IL K–3, RL 2.3) A little helicopter exhibits bravery when he rescues two boys from a perilous boating situation.

Peet, Bill. *Cyrus the Unsinkable Sea Serpent*. Houghton Mifflin, 1975. (IL K–3, RL 4.3) Cyrus, a shy and friendly serpent, finally realizes his ambition by heroically helping voyagers through a storm and foiling dastardly pirates.

Rankin, Joan. *Scaredy Cat*. Aladdin, 1999. (IL K–3, RL 2.1) A little kitten fearfully faces scary things such as a huge figure on the wall, but when he encounters a tiny spider, he discovers a bravery deep inside himself.

Schomp, Virginia. *If You Were A Police Officer*. Benchmark Books, 1998. (IL K–3, RL 4.2) Examines the many tasks performed by police officers: the prevention of crimes, the handling of emergencies, and the enforcement of laws.

Whatley, Bruce. *Captain Pajamas*. HarperCollins, 2000. (IL K–3, RL 3.2) In the middle of the night, Brian transforms himself into Captain Pajamas, Defender of the Universe, to save his older sister Jessie from attacking aliens, but they are nowhere to be found.

Fleischman, Sid. *By the Great Horn Spoon!* Little, Brown, 1988. (IL 3–6, RL 6.2) A gentleman's gentleman from Boston flees to the wilds of California during the Gold Rush and becomes a hero.

Kelly, Zachary A. *Law Enforcement*. Rourke Corp., 1999. (IL 5–8, RL 6.2) Describes the work and importance of different kinds of law enforcement officers, discussing local and state officers, federal officers and organizations and the cooperation of private citizens.

Krensky, Stephen. *Buster Baxter, Cat Saver*. Little, Brown, 2000. (IL 3–6, RL 4.3) When Buster rescues a cat stuck in a tree he is treated like a hero, but when he begins to enjoy his celebrity a little too much, his friends devise a plan to bring him back to his old self.

Mackel, Kathy. *Eggs in One Basket*. HarperCollins, 2000. (IL 3–6, RL 4.9) With the help of two middle school classmates and a bear-like talking "dog" from the planet Sirius, seventh-grader Scott Schreiber discovers that he can be a hero in other ways than on the football field.

Mudd-Ruth, Maria. *Firefighting: Behind the Scenes*. Houghton Mifflin, 1998. (IL 3–6, RL 6.2) Explains the challenging and dangerous work performed by firefighter, the clothing they wear, and the special gear they use.

Pilkey, Dav. *The Adventures of Captain Underpants: An Epic Novel*. Blue Sky Press, 1997. (IL 3–6, RL 4.8) When George and Harold hypnotize their principal into thinking that he is the superhero Captain Underpants, he leads them to the lair of the nefarious Dr. Diaper, where they must defeat his evil robot henchmen.

Quigley, James. *Johnny Germ Head*. Holt, 1997. (IL 3–6, RL 5.9) While performing an heroic act at an amusement park, third-grader Johnny Jarvis finally confronts the fear of germs that has been his obsession ever since he was seven.

Schlein, Miriam. *The Year of the Panda*. Crowell, 1990. (IL 3–6, RL 5.3) A Chinese boy rescues a starving baby panda and, in the process, learns why pandas are endangered and what the government is doing to save them.

Sonenklar, Carol. *Mighty Boy*. Orchard, 1999. (IL 3–6, RL 5.0) When he gets a chance to meet his hero, the television character Mighty Boy, Howard Weinstein discovers his own strengths that help him handle the bully in his new fourth grade class.

Wittlinger, Ellen. *Gracie's Girl.* Simon & Schuster Books for Young Readers, 2000. (IL 3–6, RL 5.2) As she starts middle school, Bess volunteers to work on the school musical in hopes of fitting in, but when she and a friend get to know an elderly homeless woman, Bess changes her mind about what is really important.

Activities (Grades K–3)

- Brainstorm what characteristics make up a hero. Does a hero need to be famous?

- Have students create a book of "Hometown Heroes." These can include community members who help people all the time, such as police, firefighters, crossing guards, and volunteers.

- Have students create a hero collage. From newspapers and magazines, they can cut out pictures and words that portray the idea of heroism. Students then create a collage of the pictures and words.

- The U.S. Postal Service often chooses famous people to be represented on a postage stamp. Many of these people could be considered heroes. Have each student choose someone he she considers a hero and create a "Hero of the Year" stamp honoring the person. Students will need to read about the person, make a stamp honoring him or her, and write a letter that persuades the Postal Service to make a stamp.

- Invite students to imagine: "If I were a superhero, I would be _____." Ask them to create a name and qualities for their superhero. Why would they like to be this particular superhero?

Activities (Grades 4–6)

- Ask students to brainstorm what characteristics make up a hero.

- Why do some people think sports stars and movie stars are heroes? Are they? If they are, what makes them heroes?

- Have students interview people in the community who are "hometown heroes." Create a booklet or web page saluting the members of the community who give of themselves so that others can be safe, including Red Cross workers, firefighters, police officers, and church workers.

- Have students create their own bibliography of children's books that exemplify the characteristics of a hero. Annotate the bibliography and explain why each main character is a hero. Children may share their books with younger students by reading to them.

- Instruct students to choose an historical figure whom they feel is a hero. Have them research the person and write up a short paper explaining why that person is a hero.

Immigration

Immigrants are people who settle in a different country than the one they were born in. There are many reasons why people immigrate to a new country. Many are seeking a better life for themselves and their families. The United States is called the nation of immigrants. This unit will focus on stories of immigration and some of the events that shaped our country.

Booktalks (Grades K–3)

Dancing with Dziadziu

Bartoletti, Susan Campbell; ill. by Annika Nelson. Harcourt Brace, 1997. (IL K–3, RL 3.5)

Gabriella loves to dance for her grandmother Babci even though she feels she isn't as good as Babci thinks she is. As she dances, Babci shares stories of her childhood in Poland before the family came to America. Babci tells of Dziadziu—Gabriella's grandfather. Babci also tells of her family's journey to America. Share the memories with Babci and Gabriella as they remember *Dancing with Dziadziu.*

Dreaming of America: An Ellis Island Story

Bunting, Eve; ill. by Ben Stahl. BridgeWater Books, 2000. (IL K–3, RL 3.8)

As Annie Moore and her young brothers stand on the deck of the ship, they see Ireland fading into the distance. They are on their way to America to join their parents, who emigrated years before. Annie is excited about her new life but sad about leaving her aunt and uncle back in Ireland. The story tells of the children's life aboard ship and their arrival at Ellis Island. They arrive on January 1, 1892. It is Annie's 15 birthday. Journey with Annie and her brothers in *Dreaming of America.*

How Pizza Came to Queens

Khalsa, Dayal Kaur. Random House, 1995. (IL K–3, RL 3.5)

In May's town, before there were frozen pizzas and take-out pizza and pizzerias, there was hardly anything good to eat. But that all changes when Mrs. Pellegrino arrives from Italy. She sniffs the air and becomes sad. Mrs. Pellegrino speaks no English, so the children cannot ask her what is wrong. They all think she is homesick and work hard to cheer her up. They put on plays and catch fireflies for her, but she never seems really happy, because there is "No pizza." Finally, May and her friends think of a sure-fire way to cheer up Mrs. Pellegrino and discover a new delicious food, too. Find out what life was like before pizza and *How Pizza Came to Queens.*

Faraway Home

Kurtz, Jane. Gulliver Books, 2000. (IL K–3, RL 3.5)

Desta is very sad when she learns that her father will be going back to Ethiopia to visit his sick mother. Desta has never been to Ethiopia, but she knows she will miss her father a lot.

To make her feel better, her father tells stories about his childhood. He tells of not wearing shoes to school, having no electricity in his house, and seeing the wild animals that lived nearby. It is obvious to Desta that her father misses his homeland a lot. Then Desta begins to think that her father will not want to come back to America once he is home again. Join Desta as she learns about life in Ethiopia and learns about her father's love.

Yoko

Wells, Rosemary. Hyperion Books for Children, 1998. (IL K–3, RL 2.5)

Yoko's mother packs all her favorite foods for her to bring to school for lunch. She prepares a special meal of rice spread over a bamboo mat with lots of special foods inside. At lunchtime, the children all unpack their lunches and start to eat. When one of the children notices the sushi and seaweed in Yoko's lunch, he makes fun of her. All the other children soon join in. Yoko is sad the rest of the day. Then the teacher has a great idea. She sends a note home to the parents inviting them to share an international food during International Food Day at Hilltop School. Will anyone try Yoko's sushi? Find out in *Yoko* by Rosemary Wells.

Booktalks (Grades 4–6)

So Far from Home: The Diary of Mary Driscoll, An Irish Mill Girl (Dear America Series)

Denenberg, Barry. Scholastic, 1997. (IL 5–8, RL 3.5)

This fictionalized diary tells the story of Mary Driscoll's journey from Ireland to Lowell, Massachusetts, where she goes to work in the woolen mills. The mill worker's life in the 1840s is not exactly the life of luxury. The girls work long days under difficult conditions. Find out what life was like *So Far from Home*.

Hello, My Name Is Scrambled Eggs

Gilson, Jamie. Lothrop, Lee & Shepard, 1985. (IL 3–6, RL 4.6)

Harvey Trumble is looking forward to the arrival of the Nguyen family. Harvey's church is sponsoring the family, but their apartment is not ready yet. Until it is, they will stay with Harvey's family. Harvey can't wait to meet 12-year-old Tuan. He and Harvey will be in the same class. Harvey wants to "Americanize" Tuan and have him as a friend. When Tuan arrives, the other boys in the class make fun of him and try to get Harvey to dump him. In the end, Harvey and Tuan learn what it is to be true to yourself and your beliefs. Find out what happens to the boys in *Hello, My Name Is Scrambled Eggs* by Jamie Gilson.

Letters from Rifka

Hesse, Karen. Holt, 1992. (IL 3–6, RL 5.1)

Young Rifka joins her family on a journey that will take them away from their home in Russia. They are on their way to America. Rifka tells her story in a series of letters to her cousin Tovah. Rifka tells of their dangerous escape from Russia and of the people they meet along the way. When the family catches typhus, Rifka is sure the journey will not continue. Fortunately, the family survives and continues their travels—but without Rifka. She has contracted ringworm and must stay behind. When she finally is well enough to travel, she boards a ship to America. She is detained at Ellis Island, though, because she does not look well. Will Rifka be able to join her family in America, or will she be sent back to Russia? To find out, read *Letters from Rifka*.

Shannon: A Chinatown Adventure, San Francisco, 1880 (Girlhood Journeys)

Kudlinski, Kathleen V. Aladdin Paperbacks, 1996. (IL 3–6, RL 3.5)

Shannon can hardly believe her eyes when she sees her new home in San Francisco. Her family would never be able to live in such a fine house if they had stayed in Ireland. The long journey from her old home to her new home seems to be worth the sacrifices. Shannon and her siblings must learn to get along in this new place. They learn about different customs and different lifestyles. When Shannon wanders into Chinatown, she is appalled at the frightening site she finds, where a young Chinese girl is being held as a slave. Shannon decides to help her. Will Shannon be successful, or will her impulsiveness get her into trouble? Read *Shannon* to find out.

Dreams in the Golden Country: The Diary of Zipporah Feldman, a Jewish Immigrant Girl (Dear America Series)

Lasky, Kathryn. Scholastic, 1998. (IL 5–8, RL 4.8)

This is the fictionalized diary of 12-year-old Zipporah "Zippy" Feldman. Zippy and her family have escaped from Russia and have settled in New York in 1902. Life is hard for the new immigrants. Zippy is put into a young grade because her English isn't very good. She dreams of becoming an actress and finds work as a prop girl in a Yiddish theater. Through good times and bad, the family struggles to hold on to their Jewish faith, although it is not certain whether they will succeed. Will the new country tear down their traditions? Can Zippy succeed in her life? To find out, read *Dreams in the Golden Country* by Kathryn Lasky.

Book List (Grades K–3)

Bunting, Eve. *A Picnic in October*. Harcourt Brace, 1999. (IL K–3, RL 4.3) A boy finally comes to understand why his grandmother insists that the family come to Ellis Island each year to celebrate Lady Liberty's birthday.

Cech, John. *My Grandmother's Journey*. Aladdin Paperbacks, 1998. (IL K–3, RL 4.8) A grandmother tells the story of her eventful life in early twentieth-century Europe and her arrival in the United States after World War II.

Hanson, Regina. *The Tangerine Tree*. Clarion, 1995. (IL K–3, RL 3.8) When Papa announces that he must leave Jamaica to work in America, Ida is heartbroken until he tells her a secret.

Joosse, Barbara M. *The Morning Chair*. Clarion, 1995. (IL K–3, RL 4.2) Bram and his family leave their small brick house in Holland and travel to a new life in New York City.

Levine, Ellen. *I Hate English!* Scholastic Inc., 1989. (IL K–3, RL 1.8) When her family moves to New York from Hong Kong, Mei Mei finds it difficult to adjust to school and learn the alien sounds of English.

Molnar-Fenton, Stephan. *An Mei's Strange and Wondrous Journey*. DK Ink, 1998. (IL K–3, RL 3.5) Six-year-old An Mei tells the story of how she was born in China and came to live in America.

Pomeranc, Marion Hess. *The American Wei*. A. Whitman, 1998. (IL K–3, RL 2.8) When Wei Fong loses his first tooth while going to his family's naturalization ceremony, many soon-to-be Americans join in the search.

Rael, Elsa. *What Zeesie Saw on Delancey Street*. Simon & Schuster Books for Young Readers, 1996. (IL K–3, RL 2.8) A young Jewish girl living on Manhattan's Lower East Side attends her first "package party" where she learns about the traditions of generosity, courage, and community among Jewish immigrants in the early 1900s.

Sandin, Joan. *The Long Way Westward*. HarperTrophy, 1992. (IL K–3, RL 2.3) Relates the experiences of two young brothers and their family, immigrants from Sweden, from their arrival in New York through the journey to their new home in Minnesota.

Tarbescu, Edith. *Annushka's Voyage*. Clarion, 1998. (IL K–3, RL 4.8) The Sabbath candlesticks given to them by their grandmother when they leave Russia help two sisters make it safely to join their father in New York.

Book List (Grades 4–6)

Castilla, Julia Mercedes. *Emilio*. Piñata Books, 1999. (IL 3–6, RL 4.9) A young immigrant from Central America finds it difficult to learn English and adjust to life in the big city of Houston, Texas.

Cohen, Barbara. *Molly's Pilgrim*. Lothrop, Lee & Shepard Books, 1998. (IL 3–6, RL 2.8) Told to make a Pilgrim doll for the Thanksgiving display at school, Molly is embarrassed when her mother tries to help her out by creating a doll dressed as she herself was dressed before leaving Russia to seek religious freedom.

Hest, Amy. *When Jessie Came Across the Sea*. Candlewick Press, 1997. (IL 3–6, RL 3.5) A 13-year-old Jewish orphan reluctantly leaves her grandmother and immigrates to New York City, where she works for three years sewing lace and earning money to bring Grandmother to the United States, too.

Moss, Marissa. *Hannah's Journal: The Story of an Immigrant Girl*. Harcourt, Inc., 2000. (IL 3–6, RL 4.3) In the Russian shtetl where she and her family live, Hannah is given a diary for her tenth birthday, and in it she records the dramatic story of her journey to America.

Ross, Lillian Hammer. *Sarah, Also Known as Hannah*. A. Whitman, 1994. (IL 3–6, RL 4.5) When 12-year-old Sarah leaves the Ukraine for America in her sister's place, she must use her sister's passport and her sister's name, Hannah.

Sachs, Marilyn. *Call Me Ruth*. Beech Tree Books, 1995. (IL 3–6, RL 5.5) The daughter of a Russian immigrant family, newly arrived in Manhattan in 1908, has conflicting feelings about her mother's increasingly radical union involvement.

Shaw, Janet Beeler. *Meet Kirsten, an American Girl*. Pleasant Co., 1986. (IL 3–6, RL 4.1) Nine-year-old Kirsten and her family experience many hardships as they travel from Sweden to the Minnesota frontier in 1854.

Shefelman, Janice Jordan. *A Paradise Called Texas*. Eakin Press, 1983. (IL 3–6, RL 5.0) Searching for a better life, Mina and her parents leave their German fatherland in 1845 and sail to Texas, where they find hardship, tragedy and adventure.

Woodruff, Elvira. *The Memory Coat*. Scholastic Press, 1999. (IL 3–6, RL 6.2) In the early 1900s, two cousins leave their Russian shtetl with the rest of their family to come to America, hopeful that they will all pass the dreaded inspection at Ellis Island.

Woodruff, Elvira. *The Orphan of Ellis Island: A Time-Travel Adventure*. Scholastic, 1997. (IL 3–6, RL 5.5) During a school trip to Ellis Island, Dominick Avaro, a 10-year-old foster child, travels back in time to 1908 Italy and accompanies two young emigrants to America.

Activities (Grades K–3)

- Discuss immigration with the students. Ask if they know what country their ancestors came from. Students may know of different ancestors that have come from several different countries. Keep a list on the board.

- Often, immigrants are discriminated against because of the way they talk or dress. Discuss with students how it would feel to go to a new place where you were not accepted.

- Have students construct a culture quilt using either paper or fabric. Each square should represent the student's cultural background. The squares can be put together to make a classroom quilt. Explain how all the cultures come together to make one.

- Have students make a "Who Am I?" collage using photographs, magazine cutouts, drawings, writing, and so on.

- Discuss the cultural origin of popular foods such as pizza, tacos, pita sandwiches, and shish kabobs. Have an international food day with various booths where children will share foods from a particular culture or from many cultures.

Activities (Grades 4–6)

- Lead a discussion on the concept of culture. Students should reflect on traditions and values. How does immigration affect the culture of a country?

- Ask students to find out where their ancestors came from. How many generations of their family have lived in the United States? Or are they Native Americans? Ask students to research an ancestor's country of origin. What factors may have contributed to their emigration? How might they have been greeted when they immigrated? Students will create an ancestor map, a world map on which each student marks the country of their ancestors. Ask students to discuss the distribution of the marks. Is there a reason some countries are more heavily represented than others?

- Plan an international day in your classroom. Students can bring in food, traditional dress, and other items that help others to better understand their cultural heritage. Students can invite parents, grandparents and other community members to share in the day.

- Have students make posters representing different cultures. Students may use magazine clippings, drawings, fabric, and other materials.

- Have students create a multicultural calendar for the classroom. Students will mark important holidays and celebrations from around the world.

Middle Ages

Knights in shining armor. Damsels in distress. Fire-breathing dragons needing to be slayed. King Arthur and Camelot. These are all images of the Middle Ages. Of course, not all the images are based on reality. In these books, children will be exposed to the Middle Ages—both real and imaginary. They will meet knights and damsels and, yes, even some dragons. Children love learning about this time in history.

Booktalks (Grades K–3)

The Royal Nap

Black, Charles C. Viking, 1995. (IL K–3, RL 4.2)

Have you ever had the hiccups and just couldn't stop? Did you try all the strange remedies that your friends suggested? Well, that's just what happened to poor Gerald the pot scrubber. Gerald worked in the castle of King Gordo. King Gordo just had to take a nap every afternoon. Everyone in the castle had to be really quiet, because the King heard everything. When Gerald's hiccups kept the king awake, Gerald was banished to the Cold and Snowy Land. Will Gerald ever be allowed back to the castle? Will King Gordo get his afternoon nap? To find out, read *The Royal Nap* by Charles C. Black.

Into the Castle

Crebbin, June; ill. by John Bendall-Brunell. Candlewick Press, 1996. (IL K–3, RL 2.8)

Could it be true? Could a monster be living in the castle? That's what five friends set out to discover. They explore the castle, looking for the monster. When they reach the dungeon, they think they see something. Do they? Is it the monster? Find out—if you dare—by going *Into the Castle.*

The Knight Who Was Afraid To Fight.

Hazen, Barbara Shook; ill. by Toni Goffe. Dial Books for Young Readers, 1994. (IL K–3, RL 2.6)

I'm sure you've heard stories of brave knights from the Middle Ages. They slew dragons and saved damsels in distress. They were fearless. Except for Sir Fred. Everyone thought he was brave and fearless. Whenever there was a dragon to be slayed or a lady to rescue, he was always there. The fair young Lady Wendylyn was in love with her brave knight. Another knight at the castle, Melvin the Miffed, hated Sir Fred. He didn't think Sir Fred was brave at all, and he set out to prove it. When Melvin the Miffed challenged Sir Fred to a duel, Sir Fred tried everything he can think of to get out of it. Unfortunately, when someone throws down his or her glove, you simply have to fight. Melvin the Miffed got ready for the duel by putting a poison tip on the end of his sword. What will happen to poor Sir Fred? Will everyone find out about him not wanting to fight? Will Lady Wendylyn leave him for another knight who really is brave? To find out, read *The Knight Who Was Afraid to Fight* by Barbara Shook Hazen.

We Just Moved!

Krensky, Stephen; ill. by Larry DiFiori. Scholastic Inc., 1998. (IL K–3, RL 1.5)

Have you ever moved to a new home? Do you remember what it was like? Do you remember how you felt? Some of these same feelings are felt by the young boy in this book. When his family moves to a bigger castle, he finds that some things about life in the new place are different and some things are the same. Find out what types of things he needs to pack. Will he ever feel at home in the new castle? Will he get over the feeling of loss? Find out in *We Just Moved!* by Stephen Krensky.

Katie and the Mona Lisa

Mayhew, James. Orchard Books, 1999. (IL K–3, RL 4.4)

Have you ever been to an art museum? Some people love to stroll around and look at the marvelous paintings hanging on the walls. Katie is one of those people. When she sees the famous da Vinci painting Mona Lisa, she decides to try to cheer up the sad lady in the painting. While her grandmother takes a break from walking around the museum, Katie persuades Mona Lisa to leave her painting. Together, Katie and Mona Lisa step in and out of famous paintings all through the museum. They learn a great deal about the events that happened in the Renaissance time period. They also learn about the famous artists of the Renaissance. Do you want to learn more about them? You won't be disappointed with *Katie and the Mona Lisa* by James Mayhew.

Booktalks (Grades 4–6)

The Shakespeare Stealer

Blackwood, Gary. Dutton Children's Books, 1998. (IL 5–8, RL 5.5)

Young Widge is an orphan growing up in 16th century England. He spends his first seven years in an orphanage and sometimes allows himself to dream about having a family and friends. At age seven, he is apprenticed to Dr. Bright, who is anything but a kind man. Dr. Bright has developed a form of shorthand writing and is determined that Widge master it. This shorthand allows Widge to write down what people are saying as they are saying it. Widge is a very bright young man, and he is able to master the shorthand in about a year. When Widge is about 14 years old, he is sold to a new master who is only interested in Widge's shorthand ability. This master is in charge of a troupe of actors who need new plays to perform. The new master sends Widge to London to steal a play by William Shakespeare. He is to attend the play and write down every word and give it to his new master. Widge knows that this is wrong, but how can he say no—especially to a man who threatens to kill him if he doesn't get the play? Along the way, Widge makes new friends and learns much about growing up.

Catherine, Called Birdy

Cushman, Karen. Clarion, 1994. (IL 3–6, RL 6.7)

The year is 1290, and 14-year-old Catherine begins her diary by writing: "I am bit by fleas and plagued by family. That is all there is to say." But Catherine does indeed have more to say. Her diary becomes her confidant through which we witness life in Middle Ages. Catherine loves birds, and everyone calls her Birdy. Birdy's father is determined to find a rich husband for her, but Birdy is determined never to marry. Follow Birdy as she enjoys life and avoids suitors in *Catherine, Called Birdy* by Karen Cushman.

Juliet: A Dream Takes Flight, England, 1339 (Girlhood Journeys)
Kirwan, Anna. Aladdin, 1996. (IL 3–6, RL 4.8)

Juliet and Marguerite are best friends. They are almost like sisters. There is a big difference, though. Marguerite is the daughter of the Lord of the Manor. Someday she will be the Lady of Rose Briar. Juliet is a commoner. Her father is a freeman who works for Marguerite's father. When word arrives that Marguerite is to leave the manor, Juliet is happy for her friend but sad for herself. She understands that this time would have to come sooner or later, but she doesn't want her friend to leave. To make her day even worse, her young brother Alban has accidentally let the prize falcon out of his shed, and Juliet sets out to find it and bring it back. After all, in Middle Ages England, a person responsible for the loss of a valuable falcon can be put to death. Find out if that happens to Alban in *Juliet: A Dream Takes Flight, England, 1339* by Anna Kirwan.

Elizabeth I, Red Rose of the House of Tudor (The Royal Diaries)
Lasky, Kathryn. Scholastic, 1999. (IL 5–8, RL 4.8)

I am the forgotten princess. I write this diary so that I can be perfectly honest with someone. It is not a good idea to be too honest around the royal court. My father is King Henry VIII, and the year is 1544. My father is now married to his sixth wife. I have an older sister, Mary. She is not quite right in the head and torments me at times. My brother is younger but it is he who is destined to rule England one day. Father used to want me to rule, but now he doesn't even acknowledge me at times. As it stands, I will never rule England. Edward is first in line, Mary is next and then I. I feel that I would be a good queen but will never get the chance. This diary will record my thoughts and my adventures as the forgotten princess. If you'd like to learn more about me, read *Elizabeth I, Red Rose of the House of Tudor* by Kathryn Lasky.

The Squire's Tale
Morris, Gerald. Houghton Mifflin, 1998. (IL 5–8, RL 5.5)

Young Terence never expected much adventure in his life. He had been left at a hermitage after his mother died. Trevisant, the hermit, is an interesting character. He has the ability to see into the future but he can't remember the past. When a stranger named Gawain arrives in the woods, Trevisant tells Terence that he must go and become squire to Gawain. Terence doesn't want to leave but knows better than to disobey the hermit. Gawain and Terence set off to join King Arthur's court. Neither knows what adventures await them. There are duels with other knights and encounters with hags and faeries. Join Terence as he shares *The Squire's Tale*.

Daly, Niki. *Bravo, Zan Angelo!: A Commedia Dell'arte Tale with Story & Pictures*. Farrar, Straus & Giroux, 1998. (IL K–3, RL 4.4) In Renaissance Venice, Angelo, longing to be as famous a clown as his grandfather, decides to do something special with his small part in his grandfather's commedia dell'arte production during Carnival.

dePaola, Tomie. *The Knight and the Dragon*. Putnam, 1980. (IL K–3, RL 3.5) A knight who has never fought a dragon and an equally inexperienced dragon prepare to meet each other in battle.

Gerrard, Roy. *Sir Cedric Rides Again*. Farrar, Straus & Giroux, 1998. (IL K–3, RL 4.7) Sir Cedric's vacation in Jerusalem with his family and servants is interrupted when his wife, Lady Matilda, and daughter, Edwina the Fair, are kidnapped by evil Abdul the Heavy.

Leigh, Susannah. *Puzzle Castle*. Usborne, EDC Publishing, 1993. (IL K–3, RL 4.5) Follow Sophie, a brave knight, on her adventures through Puzzle Castle, and meet Sophie's friends—Cecil, a friendly ghost, Jester Jim, and Titus the Timid.

Lofgren, Ulf. *Alvin the Knight*. Carolrhoda Books, 1992. (IL K–3, RL 5.3) When Alvin visits a museum and sees an exhibit of medieval costumes, he is suddenly drawn into an imaginary adventure where he gets the opportunity to prove his skill as a knight in a medieval land of kings and castles.

Morrison, Taylor. *Antonio's Apprenticeship: Painting a Fresco in Renaissance Italy*. Holiday House, 1996. (IL K–3, RL 2.9) As an apprentice in his uncle's studio, Antonio learns that creating beautiful frescoes for a Florentine chapel demands tedious chores, long hours, and unending patience.

Thomas, Shelley Moore. *Good Night, Good Knight*. Dutton Children's Books, 2000. (IL K–3, RL 1.0) A good knight helps three little dragons who are having trouble getting to sleep.

Tucker, Kathy. *Do Knights Take Naps?* A. Whitman, 2000. (IL K–3, RL 3.0) Rhyming text explores what it means to be a knight, what he wears, and what he does for fun.

Weinberger, Kimberly. *Quest for Camelot*. Scholastic, 1998. (IL K–3, RL 5.4) Kayley and Garrett travel to the Forbidden Forest to rescue Excalibur and return it to King Arthur so that he can claim his rightful place as the king of Camelot.

Wynne-Jones, Tim. *The Hunchback of Notre Dame*. Orchard Books, 1997. (IL K–3, RL 5.5) A retelling of the tale, set in medieval Paris, of Quasimodo, the hunchbacked bellringer of Notre Dame Cathedral, and his struggles to save the beautiful gypsy dancer Esmeralda from being unjustly executed.

Book List (Grades 4–6)

Bulla, Clyde Robert. *The Sword in the Tree*. HarperTrophy, 2000. (IL 3–6, RL 2.2) After he and his mother flee for their lives, a young boy goes to King Arthur for help in winning back his family's castle from his wicked uncle, and discovers that his father is still alive.

Cushman, Karen. *Matilda Bone*. Clarion, 2000. (IL 5–8, RL 6.1) Fourteen-year-old Matilda, an apprentice bonesetter and practitioner of medicine in a village in medieval England, tries to reconcile the various aspects of her life, both spiritual and practical.

De Angeli, Marguerite. *The Door in the Wall*. Doubleday, 1989. (IL 3–6, RL 6.5) A crippled boy in 14th-century England proves his courage and earns recognition from the king.

Kirwan, Anna. *Juliet: Midsummer at Greenchapel, England, 1340*. Aladdin Paperbacks, 1997. (IL 3–6, RL 7.5) On the day before Midsummer Eve in England in 1340, 11-year-old Juliet accompanies Gil on a trip to get medicine for a wounded falcon while hoping to arrive home in time for the fun.

Morris, Gerald. *The Savage Damsel and the Dwarf*. Houghton Mifflin, 2000. (IL 5–8, RL 6.4) Lynet, a feisty young woman, journeys to King Arthur's court to find a champion to rescue her beautiful older sister. She is joined in her quest by a clever dwarf and a bold kitchen knave, neither of whom are what they seem.

Morris, Gerald. *The Squire, His Knight & His Lady*. Houghton Mifflin, 1999. (IL 5–8, RL 5.3) After several years at King Arthur's court, Terence, as Sir Gawain's squire and friend, accompanies him on a perilous quest that tests all their skills and whose successful completion could mean certain death for Gawain.

Morrison, Taylor. *The Neptune Fountain: The Apprenticeship of a Renaissance Sculptor*. Holiday House, 1997. (IL 3–6, RL 5.5) In 17th-century

Rome, 15-year-old Marco is excited to be apprenticed to a famous sculptor but soon discovers that he has much to learn before he is allowed to touch a piece of stone.

Quindlen, Anna. *Happily Ever After*. Puffin, 1999. (IL 3–6, RL 5.2) When a girl who loves to read fairy tales is transported back to medieval times, she finds that the life of a princess in a castle is less fun than she imagined.

Robertson, Bruce. *Marguerite Makes a Book*. J. Paul Getty Museum, 1999. (IL 3–6, RL 4.6) In medieval Paris, Marguerite helps her nearly blind father finish painting an illuminated manuscript for his patron, Lady Isabelle.

Activities (Grades K–3)

- Have students draw a picture of a castle. Provide pictures to give them an idea of what the castle should look like. Talk about the different parts of a castle that should be included. For background information, visit the "Castles of the World" website at *www.castles.org.*

- A favorite game for children during the Middle Ages was Blind Man's Bluff. Your students can keep the game alive! To play, one child is blindfolded and stands in the middle of a circle of children. The children gently tap the blindfolded child, who must then guess who did the tapping. If he/she guesses correctly, the child who did the tapping is "it."

- Music was very important during the Middle Ages. Minstrels often traveled around the countryside, entertaining as they went. The songs they sang were often news from around the area. Have students make an instrument called a psaltery (SALL-turry) out of a shoebox. Take the lid off the shoebox. Tape aluminum foil around the box. Wrap elastic bands around the box. Students will play their psaltery by strumming it with their fingertips.

- During the Middle Ages, ships traveling long distances needed a way to tell which direction they were heading, since they had no landmarks to guide them. The compass was a wonderful invention that helped the sailors find their way. Have students build a simple compass that will point north. Materials needed include a nail, a cork or piece of Styrofoam, a small magnet, and a plastic or glass dish filled with water. Students should poke the nail through the cork so that it protrudes from both ends. Pull the nail over the magnet several times. Place in the shallow dish of water. The compass will point north!

- Brainstorm the characteristics of a knight of the Round Table. Have students use library materials to find out what was expected of a knight.

Activities (Grades 4–6)

- Direct students to research castles of the Middle Ages and prepare presentations demonstrating what they learned. Questions to be answered could include: How many types of castles were there? What were their differences? How long did it take to build a castle? How many rooms were in the average castle?

- Have students research games played during the Middle Ages, including rules and materials. They can learn the games, put them together and teach them to their classmates.

- Each student can research a different artisan from the Middle Ages. Artisans include stained-glass maker, candle maker, baker, jeweler, pottery maker and blacksmith. Students can role-play their artisan to the class, complete with props.

- Students can work in groups, each group creating a life-size person representing a character from the Middle Ages, such as serf, knight, jester, royalty, or scholar. They should include a narrative that explains who the character represents and what that person's role was in society.

- Host a medieval fair, complete with food, games, costumes, and music.

Mysteries

It was a dark and stormy night. Suddenly, a scream pierced the darkness. What has happened? Everyone loves a good mystery. There is something special about putting all the pieces together and unlocking the secret. These books all give the children clues that will let them try to figure out what the mystery is. Sometimes, the children come up with a better solution than the author has thought of. See what happens in your class.

Booktalks (Grades K–3)

Young Cam Jansen and the Baseball Mystery

Adler, David A.; ill. by Susanna Natti. Viking, 1999. (IL K–3, RL 2.2)

Cam and her friends are playing in the park. Cam isn't her real name. Cam has a fantastic memory, so her friends call her "Cam," which is short for camera. The kids get together to play a game of baseball. After one of them hits a home run, the baseball disappears. Can you figure out where they will find the ball? Read *Young Cam Jansen and the Baseball Mystery* to find out.

Grandpa's Teeth

Clement, Rod. HarperCollins, 1997. (IL K–3, RL 4.2)

Someone has stolen Grandpa's false teeth! They're nowhere to be found. The family has looked all over the house, and they simply aren't there. And to top it all off, they are the really expensive ones that Grandpa got from Switzerland. The police do their best to find the teeth. They even go so far as to insist that everyone in town smile all the time so they can check out their teeth. Anyone who refuses to smile is hauled in for a police lineup. No one can find the teeth, even when the case appears on the TV show "Unsolved Mysteries." The investigation into the crime has an unexpected effect on the town. Will they ever be able to find out who took the teeth? Will you? Read *Grandpa's Teeth* by Rod Clement to find out!

Who's in the Hall?

Hearne, Betsy; ill. by Christy Hale. Greenwillow Press, 2000. (IL K–3, RL 3.2)

This is the story of people who all live in the same apartment building. Lizzy lives on the top floor. Rowan and Ryan live on the bottom floor. Each of them has a mysterious encounter with someone who claims to be the building janitor. Who is this person who has been trying to get into the apartments? Can the kids figure it out? Can you? Read *Who's in the Hall?* to find out!

The Mystery of the Missing Red Mitten

Kellogg, Steven. Dial Books for Young Readers, 1974. (IL K–3, RL 3.2)

Have you ever lost something? What did you do to try to find it? Sometimes you need to retrace your steps to find a lost item. You can try to remember where you were when you lost it. This is what happens to the young girl in this story. She has lost her mitten and she sets off to find it. As she remembers where she has been, she starts imaging what could have happened to her mitten. She also finds lots of other lost items along the way. See if she finds her mitten in *The Mystery of the Missing Red Mitten* by Steven Kellogg.

Ducks Disappearing

Naylor, Phyllis Reynolds; ill. by Tony Maddox. Atheneum Books for Young Readers, 1997. (IL K–3, RL 3.5)

Willie and his mother are eating lunch at a restaurant while they wait for their hotel room to be ready. As Willie looks out the window, he sees a mother duck with her ducklings. Willie counts them—there are 11 ducklings in all. The next time he looks out the window to count the ducklings, there are only 10. He tells the waitress, but she isn't concerned. He looks again. Now there are only seven. One by one the ducklings are disappearing. Willie goes out to find out what is happening, and right before his eyes, one duckling disappears! Find out what is going on in *Ducks Disappearing* by Phyllis Reynolds Naylor.

Booktalks (Grades 4–6)

Stranger at the Window

Alcock, Vivien. Houghton Mifflin, 1998. (IL 5–8, RL 4.2)

Eleven-year-old Lesley is recovering from a bout of hepatitis. She has been left in the care of Aunt Amy in London. While looking out the window, Lesley sees a strange young child looking out of the attic of the house next door. Lesley knows all the children who live in the house, and this one is a stranger to her. As she attempts to learn who this child is, Lesley finds herself drawn into a mystery. See if you can figure out what is going on in the *Stranger at the Window* by Vivien Alcock.

Running Out of Time

Haddix, Margaret Peterson. Aladdin, 1995. (IL 5–8, RL 6.4)

Jessie Kayser lives in Clifton Village in 1840...or so she thinks. What Jessie doesn't know is that outside this village, it is really 1996. When a diphtheria outbreak threatens the village, Jessie's mother sends her on a dangerous mission. Jesse must leave the village to find help. If anybody finds out that she escaped, her life is in danger. Her mother tells her to contact a man who can help. He picks her up and brings her to his apartment. She decides to eavesdrop on his phone calls and learns that he has no intention of helping the villagers. He is employed by Mr. Clifton, who owns the village. It turns out that the villagers are really guinea pigs in a large experiment. If they find out, the experiment will be over. How can Jessie ever hope to go back when she now knows what is going on? To find out what happens to Jessie as well as to her family left behind in Clifton Village, read *Running Out of Time*.

From the Mixed-Up Files of Mrs. Basil E. Frankweiler

Konigsburg, E. L. Yearling, 1977. (IL 3–6, RL 5.6)

Claudia is bored with her life. Her parents don't understand her and her friends are boring. She decides to run away for a short time—just long enough for everyone to really miss her. She doesn't want to be uncomfortable during her time away from home, so she decides to take up residence in the Metropolitan Museum of Art. She also needs money, so she decides to ask her brother to run away with her, because he always has money. What

Claudia doesn't count on is being involved in an art mystery at the museum. She is determined to discover the sculptor of a magnificent statue. She learns that the former owner is Mrs. Basil E. Frankweiler and sets off to solve the mystery. See if you can solve the mystery *From the Mixed-up Files of Mrs. Basil E. Frankweiler* by E. L. Konigsburg.

Sammy Keyes and the Sisters of Mercy

Van Draanen, Wendelin. Alfred A. Knopf, 1999. (IL 5–8, RL 6.0)

Sammy got herself into a bit of trouble at school and is now required to do community service to make up for it. She's supposed to be working at the church to stay out of trouble—not to get into trouble. The problem is that right in the middle of scrubbing the dirt off the stained glass Baby Jesus, Father Mayhew accuses Sammy of stealing his favorite cross. It looks bad for Sammy because the only people in the church are Father Mayhew and Sammy. Now, how could anyone steal from Father Mayhew? He just isn't the type of person you would steal from. It's not that he's big and mean. It's just that he's so priestly. Not like some of the other priests Sammy has known. Now Sammy is on a quest to prove her innocence. When more things come up missing, the case gets more and more twisted. Who could be stealing? Could it be the homeless girl who comes to the soup kitchen, one of the nuns who run the kitchen, or even the merry Sisters of Mercy who are visiting? Find out in *Sammy Keyes and the Sisters of Mercy* by Wendelin Van Draanen.

Once Upon a Dark November

York, Carol Beach. Holiday House, 1989. (IL 3–6, RL 4.2)

Katie Allen has a crush on her freshman English teacher, Mr. Herron. She'll do anything to be close to him. She even takes a job at Mr. Herron's house helping with the housework two afternoons a week. As she helps Mrs. Herron with the dusting and polishing, she's always hopeful that she'll catch a glimpse of Mr. Herron in his study. Things change when Mrs. Herron's cousin comes for a visit. Marty is so strange. Even Mrs. Herron doesn't want him to stay. Why has Marty shown up after all these years? What is his connection with the old lady who lives across the street from Katie? Spend a dark November with Katie as she learns Marty's secret.

Book List (Grades K–3)

Adler, David A. *Young Cam Jansen and the Pizza Shop Mystery*. Viking, 2000. (IL K–3, RL 1.8) When Cam, her friend Eric, and her father stop for pizza while they are at the mall, Cam must rely on her photographic memory to locate her missing jacket.

Allen, Laura Jean. *Rollo and Tweedy and the Ghost at Dougal Castle*. HarperCollins, 1992. (IL K–3, RL 2.5) Lord Dougal asks the detective Tweedy and his assistant Rollo to solve the mystery of the ghost haunting Dougal Castle.

Bonsall, Crosby Newell. *The Case of the Hungry Stranger*. HarperTrophy, 1992. (IL K–3, RL 2.3) Soon after Wizard decided to become a private eye, he had to solve the mystery of Mrs. Meech's missing blueberry pie.

Kellogg, Steven. *The Mystery of the Stolen Blue Paint*. Dial Press, 1982. (IL K–3, RL 2.9) When her can of blue paint mysteriously disappears, Belinda is determined to find out which one of the children took it.

Platt, Kin. *Big Max*. HarperCollins, 1992. (IL K–3, RL 2.2) Big Max, the world's greatest detective, helps a king find his missing elephant.

Rylant, Cynthia. *The High-Rise Private Eyes: The Case of the Climbing Cat*. Greenwillow Books, 2000. (IL K–3, RL 2.0) The High Rise Private Eyes animal detectives try to find the cat who stole their neighbor's binoculars.

Sharmat, Marjorie Weinman. *Nate the Great*. Bantam Doubleday Dell Books for Young Readers, 1977. (IL K–3, RL 2.0) Nate the Great solves the mystery of the missing picture.

Tryon, Leslie. *Albert's Halloween: The Case of the Stolen Pumpkins*. Atheneum Books for Young Readers, 1998. (IL K–3, RL 3.9) Chief Inspector Albert the duck and his three detective assistants follow a series of clues to find the batch of pumpkins stolen from the town pumpkin patch.

Yolen, Jane. *Picnic with Piggins*. Harcourt Brace, 1988. (IL K–3, RL 2.9) A picnic in the country becomes the stage for a mystery that turns out to be a birthday surprise.

Yolen, Jane. *Piggins*. Harcourt Brace, 1987. (IL K–3, RL 3.5) During a dinner party, the lights go out and Mrs. Reynard's beautiful diamond necklace is stolen, but Piggins the butler quickly discovers the thief.

Book List (Grades 4–6)

Adler, David A. *Cam Jansen and the Ghostly Mystery*. Puffin Books, 1998. (IL 3–6, RL 3.2) Cam uses her photographic memory to catch a thief disguised as a ghost.

Banks, Lynne Reid. *The Mystery of the Cupboard*. Morrow Junior Books, 1993. (IL 3–6, RL 6.1) After the family moves to a country house recently inherited by his mother, Omri finds many secrets revealed to him when he accidentally discovers the link between the house and the magic cupboard.

Bunting, Eve. *Coffin on a Case*. HarperCollins, 1993. (IL 3–6, RL 5.2) Twelve-year-old Henry Coffin, the son of a private investigator, helps a gorgeous high school girl in her dangerous attempt to find her kidnapped mother.

Conford, Ellen. *A Case for Jenny Archer*. Little, Brown, 1988. (IL 3–6, RL 4.5) After reading three mysteries in a row, Jenny becomes convinced that the neighbors across the street are up to no good and decides to investigate.

Fleischman, Sid. *Jim Ugly*. Bantam Doubleday Dell Books for Young Readers, 1993. (IL 3–6, RL 5.8) The adventures of 12-year-old Jake and Jim Ugly, his father's part-mongrel, part-wolf dog, as they travel through the Old West trying to find out what really happened to Jake's actor father.

Giff, Patricia Reilly. *Mary Moon Is Missing*. Viking, 1998. (IL 3–6, RL 4.8) Assisted by her cat Max and her friend Cash, Minnie tries to find Mary Moon, a valuable racing pigeon that has disappeared just before a big race.

Howe, James. *Dew Drop Dead: A Sebastian Barth Mystery*. Atheneum, 1990. (IL 3–6, RL 5.5) While setting up a homeless shelter at the church, Sebastian and his friends, Corrie and David, solve the mystery of a dead man found in an abandoned inn.

Sobol, Donald J. *Encyclopedia Brown and the Case of Pablo's Nose*. Delacorte Press, 1996. (IL 3–6, RL 4.8) America's Sherlock Holmes in sneakers continues his war on crime in 10 more cases, the solutions to which are found in the back of the book.

Walker, Paul Robert. *The Sluggers Club: A Sports Mystery*. Harcourt Brace Jovanovich, 1993. (IL 3–6, RL 5.1) When baseball equipment starts disappearing from B. J.'s Little League team, he and his friends form the Sluggers Club to investigate the crime.

Yep, Laurence. *The Case of the Goblin Pearls.* HarperCollins Publishers, 1997. (IL 3–6, RL 4.8) Lily and her aunt, a Chinese American movie actress, join forces to solve the theft of some priceless pearls and stop the operator of a sweatshop in San Francisco's Chinatown.

Activities (Grades K–3)

- Ask students to create their own book jacket for the story. Talk about what elements of the story are important. How should these be portrayed on the cover?

- For any mystery book you read, have students fill in answers to the five W's: Who? What happened? Where? When? Why?

- Invite the local police to visit and explain how they investigate reports. What do they look for when they start to investigate a crime? What types of questions do they ask? Students may learn about fingerprinting.

- Introduce students to vocabulary that commonly appears in mystery stories. Ask students to draw cartoons that define each of the words as it applies to the story.

- Many times in mysteries, notes are written using letters cut out of a newspaper or magazine. Students can strengthen their letter recognition by composing notes using cutout letters.

Activities (Grades 4–6)

- Brainstorm "What is a mystery?" Are there common elements that make up the story?

- Encourage students to create their own code writing and try to decipher each others' messages. Model some simple codes, such as a code using numbers to represent letters: 1=A, 2=B, etc.

- Have students keep a mystery journal as they read. They can keep track of clues and where they think the story is taking them. Ask them to guess how the story will turn out.

- Divide the class into groups, and assign each group a character from the book. Have the students describe the character and show examples from the book to support their assessment of the character. Show how the character is connected to the central character of the book. Why is the character important to the story? How would the story change if the character's actions had changed?

- Help students write notes with invisible ink and exchange them with classmates. To create an "invisible" note, use a toothpick dipped in lemon juice to write messages on a thin piece of paper. To read the notes, students hold the paper near a light bulb until the message mysteriously appears! Brainstorm with students as to why this works. (Lemon juice is mildly acidic, and acid weakens paper. The acid remains in the paper even after the juice or vinegar dries. When the paper is held near a hot light bulb, the treated portions of the paper burn and turn brown more readily than the untreated portions.)

Pets

Most of us have had a pet sometime during our lives. Some of us cannot imagine living without a pet. There is something magical about living with a non-human. Pets don't judge or scold. For the most part, animals give us love and ask for little in return. Many of the children in your class own a pet. This unit explores different types of pets and how they interact with their humans. Students will get to know others in the class as they find they share a common love of a particular animal.

Booktalks (Grades K–3)

Arthur's New Puppy

Brown, Marc. Little, Brown, 1993. (IL K–3, RL 2.5)

Arthur has a new puppy. He and D. W. love the puppy, but they are discovering the downside of owning a pet. The new puppy is not housebroken. He has accidents all over the house—even on Arthur's lap. Not only that, but he also chews everything in sight. He ruins the new curtains, toys and even Arthur's dog training book. Can Arthur train the new puppy before his parents banish the dog to the garage? To find out, read *Arthur's New Puppy* by Marc Brown.

Roll Over, Rosie

Enell, Trinka. Clarion, 1992. (IL K–3, RL 2.7)

Do any of you have a pet? Maybe a dog? Well, have you ever tried to teach your dog to do a trick? Was it easy to do? Usually it's not that easy. You have to be very patient and repeat yourself over and over again. The young girl in this story is trying to teach her dog, Rosie, to roll over. She tries everything she can think of to get Rosie to roll over. She tries being nice and offering praise, giving treats, scolding and even threatening to give Rosie a bath. Nothing seems to work—or does it? Keep saying *Roll Over, Rosie.*

I Am the Dog, I Am the Cat

Hall, Donald; ill. by Barry Moser. Dial Books, 1994. (IL K–3, RL 3.9)

They say there are dog people and there are cat people. How many of you have dogs? How many have cats? OK, now how many of you have both? I have both, and I love seeing the difference in their behavior. I also love to watch them play together. In this book, the cat and dog explain how they see the world. They talk of their differences, their similarities and their views of each other. I think you'll recognize your own pet in *I Am the Dog, I Am the Cat* by Donald Hall.

The Snow Cat

Khalsa, Dayal Kaur. Clarkson Potter, 1992. (IL K–3, RL 3.0)

Can you imagine what it must be like to live all alone with no one else around? What about living in the woods in the winter with not a soul to talk to? Little Elsie lives this way. She prays for a cat to keep her company. There is not enough food to feed a real cat, so Elsie prays for a snow cat that will not get hungry. One night, her prayers are answered and a snow cat comes down from the sky during a storm. God warns Elsie to keep the cat outside and not bring it in by the fire. Find out what happens when Elsie forgets her promise in *The Snow Cat*.

Go Home! The True Story of James the Cat

Meggs, Libby Phillips. Albert Whitman & Co., 2000. (IL K–3, RL 2.0)

Have you ever had a strange cat show up in your yard? Did you shoo it away? That's what people usually do. That's what happens in this story. James the cat doesn't know where home is, but people keep telling him to go there. All he knows is that he must have had a home once because he has a collar on and vaguely remembers being loved. Now the collar is too small and he is having trouble eating. He is all on his own and he's scared. How will James survive? Will James find a home before it's too late? To find out, read *Go Home! The True Story of James the Cat*.

Booktalks (Grades 4–6)

Because of Winn-Dixie

DiCamillo, Kate. Candlewick Press, 2000. (IL 3–6, RL 5.8)

"My name is India Opal Buloni, and last summer my daddy, the preacher, sent me to the store for a box of macaroni-and-cheese, some white rice, and two tomatoes, and I came back with a dog." So begins the story of young India and her life in a new town. It's not easy moving to a new town and trying to make friends. When India meets a stray dog, she knows right away that she has found a true friend. She names the dog Winn-Dixie after the supermarket she found him in. Winn-Dixie is big, mangy, and perhaps the ugliest dog India has ever seen. But when he smiles, his whole body smiles. India has never known a dog who could smile, but this one sure could. Join India and Winn-Dixie as they make friends with some of the unusual characters in Naomi, Florida. It seems to India that every good thing that happens to her that summer happens *Because of Winn-Dixie*.

Nightwalkers

Morris, Judy K. HarperCollins, 1996. (IL 3–6, RL 4.8)

What would you do if an elephant came to your window at night? James couldn't believe it was happening. The elephant he saw at the zoo that afternoon was at his window. The elephant's trunk searched the room until it found James's leg. Then Daisy wrapped her trunk around the leg and pulled James out the window. The next thing he knew, he was riding an elephant through the streets of Washington, DC. The elephant returned the next night and the next night. This certainly is not the kind of animal you can keep as a pet. Who would believe how James spent his nights? Certainly not his new foster parents. His social worker wouldn't either. But James knew that he had to help the elephant find what she spent every night searching for. He would have to become one of the *Nightwalkers*.

Shiloh

Naylor, Phyllis Reynolds. Atheneum Books for Young Readers, 1991. (IL 3–6, RL 5.7)

Marty is an 11-year-old boy living in rural West Virginia with his parents and two sisters. The family is a close one, and Marty would never think of disobeying his parents. While walking near the woods one day, Marty comes across a beagle who is hiding in the bushes. He won't come out even when Marty calls to him. The dog follows Marty but won't go near him. Marty becomes convinced that the dog has been abused. Eventually, the dog begins to trust Marty and will come to him. Marty names the dog Shiloh, and the two become fast friends. However, it turns out that the dog belongs to a neighbor, and Marty has to return the dog. Shiloh runs away again and comes to Marty. Now Marty faces a real dilemma. He knows he can't keep the dog because his family can't afford to feed him. He also knows that Shiloh rightfully belongs to his neighbor, and he knows that the neighbor is abusing the dog. He must decide what to do. What would you do? What is the right thing in this situation? To find out Marty's decision, read *Shiloh* by Phyllis Reynolds Naylor.

Where the Red Fern Grows

Rawls, Wilson. Delacorte, 1996. (IL 5–8, RL 6.4)

Young Billy is growing up in the Ozarks, where hunting is a way of life. He has one dream. He dreams of owning a pair of hunting coon dogs. The family is poor and certainly can't afford to buy two coon dogs, but Billy is determined. He decides to save up his money and buy the dogs himself. He doesn't tell his parents about his plans, though. He does odd jobs around the area and saves every penny in an old tin can. By the end of the summer, he has enough to buy the dogs. With his grandfather's help, he orders the dogs and picks them up in town. The dogs are named Old Dan and Little Ann, and they are Billy's pride and joy. He trains them for competition the best he can. What Billy finds is that sometimes the things your dogs teach you are more important than what you teach them. What awaits Billy and his dogs? Will they be successful at competition? What valuable lesson will Billy learn? You'll find the answers to these questions in *Where the Red Fern Grows* by Wilson Rawls.

Smart Dog

Vande Velde, Vivian. Harcourt Brace, 1998. (IL 3–6, RL 6.3)

Have you ever heard of a talking dog? Do you think it's possible for a dog to talk? Well, Amy Prochenko, a fifth grader, believes they can. She is not a very popular girl in her class until she meets Sherlock the talking dog. Sherlock has escaped from the university genetics lab. He's on the run and is desperate not to be caught. Sherlock turns Amy's life upside down as she becomes swept up in a dangerous adventure, attempting to rescue him. What will happen to Amy and Sherlock? Can Amy really hope to rescue Sherlock from the dangerous people at the lab? What can one young girl accomplish when she finds herself up against powerful people? To find out, read *Smart Dog* by Vivian Vande Velde.

Child, Lauren. *I Want a Pet*. Tricycle Press, 1999. (IL K–3, RL 1.7) A girl tries to select a pet that will not eat her, be a copycat, make too much noise, or leave dirty footprints around the house.

dePaola, Tomie. *Pancakes for Breakfast*. Scholastic, 1991. (IL K–3, no words) A little old lady's attempts to have pancakes for breakfast are hindered by a scarcity of supplies and the participation of her pets.

Keats, Ezra Jack. *Pet Show!* Aladdin Paperbacks, 1987. (IL K–3, RL 3.0) When he can't find his cat to enter in the neighborhood pet show, Archie must do some fast thinking to win a prize.

Kellogg, Steven. *Can I Keep Him?* Dial, 1976. (IL K–3, RL 4.4) Mother objects to every pet Arnold asks to keep except one—a person.

King-Smith, Dick. *Sophie Hits Six*. Candlewick Press, 1999. (IL K–3, RL 5.3) The year that Sophie turns six, she sees her cat give birth to kittens, gets a pet rabbit from her Aunt Al, and pursues her dream of acquiring a dog.

McPhail, David M. *Emma's Pet*. Puffin, 1988. (IL K–3, RL 1.6) Emma's search for a soft, cuddly pet has a surprising ending.

Noble, Trinka Hakes. *The Day Jimmy's Boa Ate the Wash*. Dial Press, 1980. (IL K–3, RL 1.9) Jimmy's boa constrictor wreaks havoc on the class trip to a farm.

Sadler, Marilyn. *The Parakeet Girl*. Random House, 1997. (IL K–3, RL 2.5) Emma tries several pets before she becomes best friends with her parakeet Henry, but she finds that friendship threatened when her brother Bruce buys another parakeet.

Wolf, Jake. *Daddy, Could I Have an Elephant?* Puffin Books, 1998. (IL K–3, RL 2.5) Despite his father's objections, Tony insists on wanting such impractical pets as an elephant, a python, or a flamingo.

Yaccarino, Dan. *An Octopus Followed Me Home*. Viking, 1997. (IL K–3, RL 1.7) When a girl brings home an octopus and wants to keep him as a pet, her daddy reminds her of the crocodile, seals, and other inappropriate animals she has already brought into the house and created chaos.

Cox, Judy. *Third Grade Pet*. Holiday House, 1998. (IL 3–6, RL 3.3) Fearing for the safety of the third grade's class pet, Cheese the rat, Rosemary takes him home in her backpack and creates chaos in the household.

Dana, Barbara. *Zucchini*. Harper & Row, 1982. (IL 3–6, RL 4.6) A painfully shy young boy befriends a homeless baby ferret and gets as much comfort as he gives.

Graeber, Charlotte Towner. *Fudge*. Pocket Books, 1988. (IL 3–6, RL 4.6) Chad's parents agree to let him take a puppy, Fudge, on a trial basis if he takes care of her.

Howe, Deborah. *Bunnicula: A Rabbit-Tale of Mystery*. Atheneum Books for Young Readers, 1999. (IL 3–6, RL 5.2) Though scoffed at by Harold the dog, Chester the cat tries to warn his human family that their foundling baby bunny must be a vampire.

Jennings, Richard W. *Orwell's Luck*. Houghton Mifflin, 2000. (IL 3–6, RL 4.5) While caring for an injured rabbit that becomes her confidant, horoscope writer, and source of good luck, a thoughtful seventh grade girl learns to see things in more than one way.

King-Smith, Dick. *Mr. Potter's Pet*. Hyperion Paperbacks for Children, 1997. (IL 3–6, RL 5.2) Mr. Potter's boring life changes considerably after he buys an unusual mynah bird.

Mowat, Farley. *Owls in the Family*. Bantam, 1981. (IL 3–6, RL 5.0) A young boy decides to raise two owlets as pets. Wol and Weeps provide fun and excitement for the boy in Saskatoon.

Naylor, Phyllis Reynolds. *Danny's Desert Rats*. Aladdin Paperbacks, 1999. (IL 3–6, RL 5.9) T. R. and Danny join their friends in forming a group called the Desert Rats, and their major mission for the summer is helping Paul keep his beloved cat despite their townhouse development's rule against pets.

Wallace, Bill. *Ferret in the Bedroom, Lizards in the Fridge*. Holiday House, 1986. (IL 3–6, RL 4.7) Liz tells her zoologist father he must get rid of all the homeless animals he keeps at their house or she'll never win the sixth-grade class presidency, but when they're gone she misses them and learns there are more important things than winning.

Weber, Susan Bartlett. *Seal Island School*. Viking, 1999. (IL 3–6, RL 3.8) On Seal Island off the coast of Maine, a place swarming with pets of all kinds, nine-year-old Pru plans to keep her teacher from leaving by finding her a dog.

Activities (Grades K–3)

- Survey students as to what types of pets they have. Keep track using a chart on the wall. What is the most popular pet in the class?

- Have students make a do/don't poster for a favorite pet. For a "Cats Do/Dogs Don't" poster, students will brainstorm things that cats can do and dogs can't: Cats meow, dogs don't; cats purr, dogs don't, and so on. Then they can make a "Dogs Do/Cats Don't" poster.

- Brainstorm what is attractive about different pets. Ask students to choose which pet they would like to be if they could. Have them explain their choice.

- Conduct a pet contest. Each student will create a poster that tells all about his/her pet. This pet can be real or imaginary. The poster will list what is special about the pet. There should be enough winning categories that each child will receive a ribbon: largest pet, smallest pet, hairiest pet, and others.

- Ask students to make up clues as to what kind of animal they are thinking about. Other students will try to guess what the animal is. (E.g.: I am furry, I like to play with string, I have sharp claws, I say meow.)

Activities (Grades 4–6)

- Survey the class to find out what pets students have. Keep a chart of the pets on the wall. Students can use graphing software on the computer to create their own charts to find out the percentages of ownership of different pets.

- Ask students to design an advertisement for their favorite pet. The advertisement should attempt to persuade others that their pet is the best.

- Help students design a flipbook that illustrates a pet moving. Use a pad of paper or make your own by stapling together 24 sheets of the same size paper. Students should draw their animal on each page with the animal in a slightly different position each time. Animate the animal by flipping the pages of the book.

- What characteristics make up the ideal pet? Ask students to create a list of the best qualities for a pet, such as loyalty, protectiveness, or cuddliness. Have them "design" their own pet using these characteristics and their knowledge of what types of animals are known for the characteristics.

- Have students, individually or as a class, write a poem about a pet.

School Days

School is something we all have in common. Our experiences may differ, though. Some children love school and some hate it. Some children are worried that they won't do well or fit in. Some are loners and some are "joiners." These books are all about the experiences of going to school. From the first day of kindergarten all through the years, children have experiences in school that will shape who they become. We all hope that children will be positively influenced by the school experience.

Booktalks (Grades K–3)

Wemberly Worried

Henkes, Kevin. Greenwillow Books, 2000. (IL K–3, RL 2.8)

Have you ever been worried about something? Sometimes our worries are little—what to wear, what to say. Sometimes our worries are big—whether we will get through a storm or an illness. Sometimes we worry about things that can't happen—will the sun not come up?...will you go down the bathtub drain? Well, Wemberly worries about everything! Her parents try to convince her that she shouldn't worry, but she can't help it. Now she is facing a big day in her life—her first day of school! She is worried about what to wear, what to say, and even what the room will smell like! Will Wemberly be able to enjoy her first day of school or should she be worried? Spend the day with Wemberly in *Wemberly Worried* by Kevin Henkes.

The Awful Aardvarks Go to School

Lindberg, Reeve; ill. by Tracey Campbell Pearson. Viking, 1997. (IL K–3, RL 4.2)

The school day looked as if it was going to be great—until the awful aardvarks arrived. You know the type. They can destroy everything in no time at all. They picked on everyone. They destroyed the classroom. Can anyone stop the awful aardvarks? To find out, read *The Awful Aardvarks Go to School* by Reeve Lindberg.

Miss Bindergarten Gets Ready for Kindergarten

Slate, Joseph; ill. by Ashley Wolff. Dutton Books, 1996. (IL K–3, RL 1.3)

Do you remember your first day of kindergarten? Do you remember getting ready? Maybe you put on brand new clothes. Maybe you packed a backpack full of school supplies. Maybe you packed your new lunch box full of good things to eat. Have you ever wondered what teachers do to get ready? This story follows Miss Bindergarten as she gets her classroom ready to welcome her brand new students. As the children get ready, so does Miss Bindergarten. To find out what the teacher does to get ready, read *Miss Bindergarten Gets Ready for Kindergarten* by Joseph Slate.

Minerva Louise at School

Stoeke, Janet Morgan. Dutton Children's Books, 1996. (IL K–3, RL 2.2)

Minerva Louise is a chicken. Sometimes she gets confused. One day she gets up before all the other chickens and decides to go for a walk. Before long, she comes across the local elementary school. She mistakes it for a fancy barn. She decides to go in and take a look. Minerva Louise sure sees things differently than you or I. She mistakes lots of the school furniture for barnyard things! When she has seen enough, she decides to go home to her own barn. What did she learn in school that she could use in the barn? To find out, read *Minerva Louise at School* by Janet Morgan Stoeke.

Timothy Goes to School

Wells, Rosemary. Viking, 2000. (IL K–3, RL 1.9)

Timothy is really excited. He is starting kindergarten. He knows just what he'll wear on the first day of school—his brand new sun suit. So off he goes feeling great about himself— that is, until he runs into Claude. Claude laughs at Timothy and tells him no one wears sun suits on the first day of school. They all wear a jacket and tie. Timothy is devastated. On the second day, Timothy wears a jacket and tie. Can you guess what happens? Claude tells Timothy that no one wears a jacket and tie on the second day of school. This goes on and on. Have you ever known anyone like Claude? Someone who thinks they know everything? Someone who makes you feel insecure? Find out how Timothy handles the situation in *Timothy Goes to School* by Rosemary Wells.

Booktalks (Grades 4–6)

Flying Solo

Fletcher, Ralph. Clarion, 1998. (IL 5–8, RL 5.5)

Have you ever sat in a class in which the teacher hasn't arrived and isn't going to? There's no substitute coming, either. What do you do? Do you go wild and take advantage of the situation? Well, that's not what happens in *Flying Solo*. When the substitute teacher doesn't show up, the kids decide to lead the class themselves. Can the students be successful? What happens when kids start *Flying Solo*?

Middle School Blues

Kassem, Lou. Houghton Mifflin, 1986. (IL 5–8, RL 4.8)

Cindy Cunningham doesn't think she really fits into her family. She's not as pretty or smart as her two sisters. She's a 12-year-old "Calamity Jane." Cindy is not looking forward to starting middle school. She isn't sure what to expect, so she goes to the library to find a book that will tell her. When she doesn't find one, she decides to keep a record of her experiences and write a book about it. On her first day of school, she is ready to drop out. She can't get her locker open, she doesn't know any of the kids, and she now has six teachers instead of just one. Read Cindy's story as she faces the many challenges and triumphs of the first year of middle school.

The Chicken Doesn't Skate

Korman, Gordon. Scholastic Press, 1996. (IL 5–8, RL 5.5)

Ah, the dreaded school science project. Mrs. Bag's sixth grade class must come up with ideas by the end of the week. When Milo Neal said he was going to do a project on "The Complete Life Cycle of a Link in the Food Chain," Mrs. Bag was delighted. After all, Milo is the son of a famous scientist, so this project has the potential to be really special. When Milo brings his project to school, the class goes wild. Milo intends to raise a chicken to adulthood right in the classroom. Everyone in the class falls in love with Henrietta the chicken and fights for the opportunity to care for her. The story is told from the point of view of several of the children. Find out how one small chicken turns a town upside down in *The Chicken Doesn't Skate* by Gordon Korman.

Standing Up to Mr. O.

Mills, Claudia. Farrar, Straus & Giroux, 1998. (IL 3–6, RL 6.3)

Have you ever had a teacher who you thought the world of? A teacher who you felt could do no wrong? Then you can understand how Maggie McIntosh feels about her biology teacher, Mr. O. He starts off each class with a joke and wears the greatest ties. Maggie thinks he's the greatest teacher ever. But what happens when that teacher does something that you think is morally wrong? Do you have the courage to say so? That's what Maggie finds herself doing when Mr. O. announces that they will be dissecting animals in biology class. At first Maggie tries to go along with the experiment. She just can't get herself to dissect an earthworm, though. Then comes the fish, and she refuses to participate. If Maggie truly believes that dissecting animals is wrong, how can she believe in Mr. O. again? Join Maggie as she comes to terms with her feelings and begins *Standing Up to Mr. O.*

Jonah the Whale

Shreve, Susan. Arthur A. Levine Books, 1998. (IL 3–6, RL 5.8)

Eleven-year-old Jonah Morrison is not having a very good year. His family has just moved to Connecticut from New York City after his dad left. Jonah is not the type of kid who makes friends easily. He isn't into sports, isn't academic, and has recently become overweight. One day, he is teased by kids who call him Jonah the whale. Jonah has a tendency to lie, and this insult puts his imagination into overdrive. He tells the kids that he has his own television show called Jonah the Whale and that he has interviewed Michael Jordan! Now all the kids want to hear the Jordan interview. How will he get out of this mess? Find out how in *Jonah the Whale.*

Book List (Grades K–3)

Brown, Marc. *Arthur's Teacher Trouble*. Little, Brown, 1986. (IL K–3, RL 3.8) Third-grader Arthur is amazed when he is chosen to be in the school spell-a-thon.

Crews, Donald. *School Bus*. Greenwillow Books, 1984. (IL K–3, RL 1.2) Follows the progress of school buses as they take children to school and bring them home again.

Gantos, Jack. *Back to School for Rotten Ralph*. HarperCollins, 1998. (IL K–3, RL 2.8) Afraid of being left alone, Rotten Ralph, the nasty red cat, follows Sarah to school and tries to prevent her from making new friends.

Howard, Elizabeth Fitzgerald. *Virgie Goes to School with Us Boys*. Simon & Schuster Books for Young Readers, 2000. (IL K–3, RL 3.0) In the post-Civil War South, a young African American girl is determined to prove that she can go to school just like her older brothers.

Maurer, Donna. *Annie, Bea, and Chi Chi Dolores: A School Day Alphabet*. Orchard Books, 1998. (IL K–3, RL 1.6) The letters of the alphabet provide a humorous look at some of the activities of young animals at school, including counting, erasing, making music, painting, and snack time.

Mills, Lauren A. *The Rag Coat*. Little Brown, 1991. (IL K–3, RL 2.8) Minna proudly wears her new coat made of clothing scraps to school, where the other children laugh at her until she tells them the stories behind the scraps.

Schwartz, Amy. *Annabelle Swift, Kindergartner*. Orchard, 1988. (IL K–3, RL 3.9) Although some of the things her older sister taught her at home seem a little unusual at school, other lessons help make Annabelle's first day in kindergarten a success.

Shannon, David. *David Goes to School*. Blue Sky Press, 1999. (IL K–3, RL 2.9) David's activities in school include chewing gum, talking out of turn, and engaging in a food fight, causing his teacher to say over and over, "No, David!"

Wells, Rosemary. *Emily's First 100 Days of School*. Hyperion Books for Children, 2000. (IL K–3, RL 3.1) Starting with number one for the first day of school, Emily learns the numbers to 100 in many different ways.

Wiesner, David. *Sector 7*. Clarion, 1999. (IL K–3, no words)While on a school trip to the Empire State Building, a boy is taken by a friendly cloud to visit Sector 7, where he discovers how clouds are shaped and channeled throughout the country.

Book List (Grades 4–6)

Cleary, Beverly. *Ramona's World*. Morrow Junior Books, 1999. (IL 3–6, RL 6.2) Follows the adventures of nine-year-old Ramona at home with big sister Beezus and baby sister Roberta and at school in Mrs. Meacham's class.

Clements, Andrew. *The Landry News: A Brand New School Story*. Aladdin Paperbacks, 2000. (IL 3–6, RL 6.1) A fifth-grader starts a newspaper with an editorial that prompts her burnt-out classroom teacher to begin really teaching again, but he is later threatened with disciplinary action as a result.

Fitzgerald, John Dennis. *The Great Brain at the Academy*. Bantam Doubleday Dell Books for Young Readers, 1988. (IL 3–6, RL 5.2) With daring exploits and moneymaking schemes, the Great Brain faces the challenge of life at a strict Catholic boarding school.

Frasier, Debra. *Miss Alaineus: A Vocabulary Disaster*. Harcourt, Inc., 2000. (IL 3–6, RL 4.6) When Sage's spelling and definition of a word reveal her misunderstanding of it to her classmates, she is at first embarrassed but then uses her mistake as inspiration for the vocabulary parade.

Giff, Patricia Reilly. *Shark in School*. Bantam Doubleday Dell Books for Young Readers, 1995. (IL 3–6, RL 3.4) When Matthew finds out from J. P., the weird girl next door, that their teacher loves to read, he worries that everyone at his new school will know he's a terrible reader.

Gorman, Carol. *Dork in Disguise*. HarperTrophy, 2000. (IL 3–6, RL 6.0) Starting middle school in a new town, brainy Jerry Flack changes his image from "dork" to "cool kid," only to discover that he'd rather be himself.

Hesse, Karen. *Just Juice*. Scholastic Signature, 1999. (IL 3–6, RL 3.5) Realizing that her father's lack of work has endangered her family, nine-year-old Juice decides that she must return to school and learn to read in order to help their chances of surviving and keeping their house.

Pilkey, Dav. *The Adventures of Captain Underpants: An Epic Novel*. Blue Sky Press, 1997. (IL 3–6, RL 4.8) When George and Harold hypnotize their principal into thinking that he is the superhero Captain Underpants, he leads them to the lair of the nefarious Dr. Diaper, where they must defeat his evil robot henchmen.

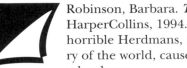

Robinson, Barbara. *The Best School Year Ever*. HarperCollins, 1994. (IL 3–6, RL 5.4) The six horrible Herdmans, the worst kids in the history of the world, cause mayhem throughout the school year.

Sachar, Louis. *Wayside School Gets a Little Stranger*. Avon Books, 1995. (IL 3–6, RL 4.3) Unusual things continue to happen in the classroom on the 30th floor of Wayside School, which was accidentally built sideways with one classroom on each story.

Activities (Grades K–3)

- Have students draw a map of their school. The map should include important areas such as the principal's office, nurse's office, cafeteria, and library. Younger students may need an outline map to label.

- Although most of us don't really like rules, we've seen through some of these books that rules are important, and it can be chaotic when students don't obey the rules. Have the students come up with A-B-C rules by using the alphabet and making a rule starting with each letter of the alphabet (e.g., A is for Always hang up your coat; B is for Be on Time, etc.). This can be done as a group project with each child assigned a letter. For the harder letters (X, Z), the class can brainstorm ideas.

- Invite students to think back to their first day of school. What memories do they have? Think about sounds, smells, and sights that were particularly impressive. They can write a list of these memories and be prepared to share them with the class.

- Design a school banner. The banner should reflect things that are important to your school or unique about the school. Brainstorm ideas for what images should be included. Students can each design their own banner.

- Have students draw a map of the classroom and label where things are: pencil sharpener, paints, cubbies.

Activities (Grades 4–6)

- Help students design a school banner, selecting and explaining the different types of symbols they think should be on the banner.

- Have students find out the history of your school. When was it built? Did it replace an old school? Was it named after someone? If so, why was that person chosen? Students can work in groups to find out different pieces of information. Compile the final report into a keepsake book.

- Students will create an acrostic poem using the name of the school, city, teacher, or team.

  Example:
  S ometimes
  C hildren
  H ave
  O nly to look to
  O thers to
  L earn about themselves.

- Have students create a memory string for important events during the school year. Use a piece of yarn for the string. Students can use buttons, paper beads or pasta beads to represent the events of the year.

- When studying new vocabulary words, ask students to guess what the words mean by how they sound. Discuss why the child thought that is what the word means. Then tell students to check the dictionary to see how close they were.

Science Fiction

Few things capture our imaginations like science fiction. Whether we are reading about living in outer space or meeting extraterrestrial beings, or imagining robots waiting on us hand and foot, science fiction knows no bounds. Children are drawn to science fiction as a way to stretch their imaginations. There are no right or wrong perspectives. Children can make up alien creatures that are friendly and helpful. They can imagine scary monsters that are out to hurt them. They can envision marvelous machines that will make our lives much more comfortable. Let the children run wild with some great science fiction books.

Booktalks (Grades K–3)

Boing-Boing the Bionic Cat

Hench, Larry L.; ill. by Ruth Denise Lear. American Ceramic Society, 2000. (IL K–3, RL 3.2)

Daniel sits on his front steps and cries. He is so sad. You see, more than anything else in the world, Daniel wants a cat. His mother has just said no again. Daniel knows she's right. He is allergic to cats. He starts to sneeze whenever he is near one. When Professor George from next door hears about Daniel's dilemma, he decides that he can help. Professor George builds robots at the local university, and he secretly works on building a robotic cat for Daniel. When it is finished, everything works fine except for one major thing! What has gone wrong? Will the Professor be able to fix it? To find out, read *Boing-Boing the Bionic Cat* by Larry L. Hench.

Alien Invasions

Kendall, Benjamin. Landmark Editions, 1993. (IL K–3, RL 3.9)

Have you ever seen something and told someone about it, and they didn't believe you? Isn't it frustrating? You try to tell them again but they just ignore you. In this story, nine-year-old Ben is the only one who can see the aliens. When he puts on his special superhero costume, he can see them clear as day. He sees them trying to sabotage his food and impersonating his parents and people at school. He decides that it is up to him to defend against the aliens. His attempts prove to be more comical than fruitful. To find out how Ben attempts to rid the world of aliens, read Benjamin Kendall's *Alien Invasions*.

My Brother Is from Outer Space

Ostrow, Vivian; ill. by Eric Brace. A. Whitman, 1996. (IL K–3, RL 2.8)

Have you ever known anyone who was just a bit different? Maybe a lot different? Did you ever imagine that they might be from outer space? Meet Alex. He is convinced that his younger brother is indeed from outer space. William is just so different from everyone else. There is no other possible explanation. Alex decides that it is up to him to break the awful news to his parents. He can't believe it when they just laugh at him. Alex sets off to prove that William is from outer space. He starts on his Book of Proof, which will prove beyond a shadow of a doubt that William is not from Earth. What does Alex find out as proof? Do you believe what he finds? Do you think William is from outer space? To find out if you're right, read *My Brother Is from Outer Space* by Vivian Ostrow.

Ned Feldman, Space Pirate

Pinkwater, Daniel. Macmillan, 1994. (IL K–3, RL 4.5)

Ned hears a strange noise coming from under the kitchen sink. What could possibly be under the sink? Never in all his years could he have expected to find Captain Bugbeard—alias Lumpy Lugo. Captain Bugbeard is a nasty little green creature who wears an eye patch and flies a Jolly Roger—the flag of a pirate. It turns out that is exactly what he is! He is a fierce space pirate. Captain Bugbeard takes Ned off to explore the universe. Together they encounter giant chickens and an aggressive Yeti. Will Ned ever see his home again? Will the Captain return him safely? You'll need to read *Ned Feldman, Space Pirate* by Daniel Pinkwater to find out.

June 29, 1999

Wiesner, David. Houghton Mifflin, 1992. (IL K–3, RL 5.3)

"The place is Ho-Ho-Kus, New Jersey. The year is 1999. On May 11, after months of careful research and planning, Holly Evans launches vegetable seedlings into the sky." Holly isn't content growing seeds inside paper cups like the rest of the class. She wants to find out the effects of extraterrestrial conditions on various vegetables. On June 29, vegetables start falling from the sky. How have they changed by being in outer space? To find out, read *June 29, 1999*.

Booktalks (Grades 4–6)

My Life Among the Aliens

Gauthier, Gail. Putnam, 1996. (IL 3–6, RL 5.2)

Will and Robby are just two ordinary kids living ordinary lives in an ordinary neighborhood. When the brothers are visited by aliens, things change. Of course, no one believes that Leo and Fred are aliens or that their dog Sandy can now talk, but Will and Robby know. One by one, more aliens come to visit Will and Robby's home. What is bringing them there? Is it really their mother's bran muffins or is it something else? Find out about *My Life Among the Aliens*.

Among the Hidden

Haddix, Margaret Peterson. Simon & Schuster, 1998. (IL 3–6, RL 5.6)

Luke is a "shadow child." He hasn't heard the term yet, but he will. Luke is living in a future time where the Population Police rule family life. It is the law that families can only have two children. Luke has two older brothers, so he must remain hidden from everyone and everything. He doesn't quite know what would happen to him if he is found out, but he is sure his parents would be punished. His life isn't too bad, though. He can work on his father's farm and get out into the sunshine—until the woods are cut down to make room for some fancy new houses. Then Luke is restricted to the house all the time. He finds that he can peek out of the attic vent and see the new houses. To his amazement, he sees movement in one of the homes long after the parents and two sons have left. Luke decides to risk going over to the house to find out if there is another third child in hiding.

What he finds will change his life forever. To discover what Luke finds in the house of the Baron, read *Among the Hidden*.

The Forgotten Door

Key, Alexander. Scholastic, 1965. (IL 3–6, RL 3.0)

This is a story about a visitor who falls upon a backwoods family and tries to figure out who he is. He's apparently had an accident and has lost his memory. The kind family slowly comes to realize that this boy comes from another planet. The family's father tells white lies to protect the boy, but these lies end up getting him further into trouble with the law. Will the boy remember who he is? Will the family be able to protect him from the authorities? To learn the fate of this boy, read *The Forgotten Door* by Alexander Key.

The Boy Who Reversed Himself

Sleator, William. Dutton, 1998. (IL 5–8, RL 6.5)

Omar is a nerd. He seems to be spying on Laura, who is just getting to be friends with Peter, a real popular boy. She doesn't need Omar around to ruin her image, but the more she hangs around Omar, the more curious she gets. Why do some of her papers have reversed lettering after Omar gets hold of them? How can he part his hair on opposite sides—all in the same day? Laura gets taken on an adventure with Omar, and later she drags Peter on a wild trip. This science fiction experience with the fourth dimension will give you a whole new dimension to think about!

House of Stairs

Sleator, William. Dutton, 1974. (IL 5–8, RL 6.0)

Peter is a 16-year-old living in an orphanage. One day he is called into the main office and taken out blindfolded. He is brought to a place so strange that he can't understand it. There are only stairs with small landings—no rooms or hallways. Soon, he is joined by four other orphans who were brought in blindfolded. The five teens wander the stairs looking for a way out. On one landing, they find a small machine that gives food—but only when Blossom sticks out her tongue. The others must depend on Blossom for food. After a while, the machine stops responding to Blossom, and the group tries other ways to get food. They make up dances and the machine responds. Each time the teens figure out how to get food, the machine changes the rules. As the teens get frustrated, they start turning on each other. The machine then demands more and more acts of anger and violence before it will give food. As they realize what is happening, they must decide if it is better to starve than become subhuman. This is a story of science misused.

Book List (Grades K–3)

Bush, Timothy. *Benjamin McFadden and the Robot Babysitter*. Crown, 1998. (IL K–3, RL 2.8) When Benjamin McFadden reprograms his Robot Babysitter to be more fun, he discovers that there is such a thing as too much fun.

Cecil, Laura. *Noah and the Space Ark*. Carolrhoda Books, 1998. (IL K–3, RL 2.8) Many years in the future, when the Earth has become too polluted to support life, Noah and his family build a space ark and take the surviving animals and plants to search for a new home.

DiTerlizzi, Tony. *Jimmy Zangwow's Out-of-This-World, Moon Pie Adventure*. Simon & Schuster Books for Young Readers, 2000. (IL K–3, RL 3.3) When Jimmy's mother won't let him have any moon pies for a snack, he takes a trip to the moon to get some.

Dorros, Arthur. *The Fungus That Ate My School*. Scholastic Press, 2000. (IL K–3, RL 3.0) While the students are home for spring vacation, the fungus they are growing in their classroom grows and grows and takes over the entire school.

Lasky, Kathryn. *Science Fair Bunnies*. Candlewick Press, 2000. (IL K–3, RL 3.0) In need of a replacement science fair project, two friends must decide whether to use their loose teeth or leave them for the Tooth Fairy.

McPhail, David M. *Tinker and Tom and the Star Baby*. Little, Brown, 1998. (IL K–3, RL 3.5) A boy and a bear find a Star Baby in their backyard and try to fix its spaceship so that it can return to its mother.

Peet, Bill. *The Wump World*. Houghton Mifflin, 1970. (IL K–3, RL 3.2) The Wump World is an unspoiled place until huge monsters bring hordes of tiny creatures from the planet Pollutus.

Pinkney, J. Brian. *Cosmo and the Robot*. Greenwillow Books, 2000. (IL K–3, RL 4.0) Cosmo, a boy living on Mars, must come up with a quick solution when his malfunctioning robot Rex threatens his sister Jewel.

Rosen, Michael. *Mission Ziffoid*. Candlewick Press, 1999. (IL K–3, RL 2.5) An exploding spaceship strands a boy on the planet Ziffoid, where he encounters an energetic and playful group of aliens.

Yolen, Jane. *Commander Toad and the Intergalactic Spy*. PaperStar, 1997. (IL K–3, RL 3.1) Commander Toad and the crew of Star Warts are asked to rout out Tip Toad, Space Fleet's greatest and most elusive spy.

Book List (Grades 4–6)

Brittain, Bill. *Shape-Changer*. HarperTrophy, 1995. (IL 3–6, RL 5.5) Two seventh-grade friends help a shape-changing policeman from the planet Rodinam as he tries to recapture an alien master criminal who can also change form.

Bunting, Eve. *Wanna Buy an Alien?* Clarion, 2000. (IL 3–6, RL 4.2) For his 11th birthday, Ben receives an offer of a ride to the planet Cham with an alien named Iku, and when the appointed meeting time arrives Ben is not sure whether he faces an exciting opportunity or horrible danger.

Cameron, Eleanor. *The Wonderful Flight to the Mushroom Planet*. Little, Brown and Co., 1954. (IL 3–6, RL 4.9) A mystery man inspires two boys to build a spaceship that takes them to the planet of Basidium to help the Mushroom people.

Coville, Bruce. *Aliens Ate My Homework*. Pocket, 1993. (IL 3–6, RL 6.0) Rod is surprised when a miniature spaceship lands in his school science project and reveals five tiny aliens, who ask his help in apprehending an interstellar criminal.

Crilley, Mark. *Akiko on the Planet Smoo*. Delacorte Press, 2000. (IL 3–6, RL 5.0) Ten-year-old Akiko has an unexpected adventure when she is whisked away to a distant planet and put in charge of the rescue mission that must search for the kidnapped Prince Froptoppit.

Etra, Jonathan. *Aliens for Breakfast*. Random House, 1988. (IL 3–6, RL 3.9) Finding an intergalactic special agent in his cereal box, Richard joins the extraterrestrial in a fight to save Earth from the Dranes, one of whom is masquerading as a student in Richard's class.

Gardiner, John Reynolds. *Top Secret*. Little, Brown and Co., 1984. (IL 3–6, RL 4.0) Despite the disapproval of his parents and his formidable science teacher, nine-year-old Allen determines to do his science project on human photosynthesis.

Lowry, Lois. *The Giver*. Houghton Mifflin, 1993. (IL 5–8, RL 5.5) Given his lifetime assignment at the Ceremony of Twelve, Jonas becomes the receiver of memories shared by only one other in his community and discovers the terrible truth about the society in which he lives.

Service, Pamela F. *Stinker from Space*. Fawcett Juniper, 1989. (IL 3–6, RL 5.3) An agent of the Sylon Confederacy who is fleeing from enemy ships crash lands on Earth, transfers his mind to the body of a skunk, and enlists the aid of two children in getting back to his home planet.

Yolen, Jane. *Commander Toad and the Voyage Home.* Putnam, 1998. (IL 3–6, RL 4.6) Commander Toad leads the lean green space machine "Star Warts" to find new worlds but runs into trouble when he sets course for home.

Activities (Grades K–3)

- Many science fiction books are about space aliens. Ask students to draw a picture of what they think a space alien might look like.

- Instruct students to write a cooperative science fiction story. Working in groups, they can brainstorm ideas for a short story. Students can write alternate sentences to complete the story.

- Invite students to write a new ending for one of the books.

- Help students build a model of a spaceship. Does it look as if it might fly? Where do the astronauts sit? How many people can travel in the ship?

- Have students rewrite the story as a play and act it out for the class.

Activities (Grades 4–6)

- Lead students in a discussion of how these books would be different if the characters were normal human beings.

- Invite students to draw the main character from a science fiction book as they imagine him or her to look.

- Many times, science fiction books show us characters that scare us. Ask students: What is it that we find scary about the creatures?

- Invite students to create a diorama of a world different from the one they know.

- There is much talk about space colonies and orbiting space stations. Have students write a short story about what life would be like living on a different planet or on a space station.

Sports

At one time or another, we are all involved in sports. Be it kickball on the school playground or a competitive soccer team, the experiences are the same. Children need to learn that rules are important in any sport—the same as they are in society. Sports can have a positive impact of the lives of children if they understand where they fit. Too much emphasis on sports can put undue pressure on children that can have a negative effect. These books show children playing different sports, learning about sportsmanship and learning about the impact that sports can have on their lives.

Booktalks (Grades K–3)

The Babe & I

Adler, David A.; ill. by Terry Widener. Gulliver Books, 1999. (IL K–3, RL 2.8)

Do you have a sports hero—someone you look up to? Sometimes sports figures affect our lives in ways we can never predict. This story takes place during a time known as The Great Depression. During the 1930s, the economy was very bad. Many people were out of work and had no money. Some lost their homes and everything they owned. This book tells the story of a young boy whose family is touched by the poverty of that time. Find out how the great Babe Ruth helps the boy and his family without even knowing it in *The Babe & I* by David Adler.

Impatient Pamela Asks: Why Are My Feet So Huge?

Koski, Mary; ill. by Dan Brown. Trellis Publishing, 1999. (IL K–3, RL 3.3)

Pamela was playing with one of her friends when he mentioned that her feet were much bigger than his. Pamela had never noticed how big her feet were before! She ran home and asked her mother why her feet were so big. Her mother told her not to worry about it. She'd grow into them eventually. But Pamela was impatient. She became so self-conscious about her feet that she wouldn't leave the house. When soccer tryouts came up, Pamela didn't want to go because her feet were too big. Maybe soccer is just what she needs. What do you think? Will Pamela try out for soccer? Will she learn to accept the size of her feet? To find out for sure, read *Impatient Pamela Asks: Why Are My Feet So Huge?* by Mary Koski.

Preston's Goal!

McNaughton, Colin. Harcourt Brace & Company, 1997. (IL K–3, RL 1.5)

Preston thinks of himself as the world's greatest soccer player. He always has a soccer ball with him. When his mother sends him to the store to buy a loaf of bread, he takes his soccer ball along. He shoots, he scores!...all the way to the store. He dribbles, he passes. All the while, he is unaware of the chaos he is causing all around him. He has really gotten on the bad side of Mr. Wolf. Find out what Preston does on the way to the store and what Mr.

Wolf decides to do to Preston in *Preston's Goal!* by Colin McNaughton.

Swish!

Martin, Bill, Jr. and Michael Sampson; ill. by Michael Chesworth. Holt, 1997. (IL K–3, RL 1.9)

Do you like playing basketball? Do you like watching it? This is the story of a very exciting basketball game. The Cardinals and Blue Jays are pretty evenly matched. The girls trade baskets back and forth. They are playing for the championship. The suspense builds until there is only one second on the clock! Which team will win? Can anyone possibly make a basket with so little time on the clock? To find out, read *Swish!* by Bill Martin, Jr. and Michael Sampson.

Zachary's Ball

Tavares, Matt. Candlewick Press, 2000. (IL K–3, RL 3.0)

Have you ever gone to a major league baseball game? There is definitely a magical feeling about it, seeing the field, the players and all the fans. You can get lost in all the fun. When Zachary's dad takes him to his first game at Fenway Park in Boston, Zachary can feel the magic. His favorite player is up to bat and suddenly, a foul ball is heading Zachary's way. Just like magic, his dad catches the ball and hands it to Zachary. In that moment, Zachary's life changes. To find out how, read *Zachary's Ball* by Matt Tavares.

Booktalks (Grades 4–6)

All-Star Fever: A Peach Street Mudders Story

Christopher, Matt. Little, Brown, 1997. (IL 3–6, RL 4.0)

How would you feel if you broke one of your parents' rules? What if you weren't caught? Would you feel guilty? When Bus Mercer gets a new dirt bike, he forgets the rules and rides it when he doesn't have permission. He feels so guilty about disobeying his parents that it begins to affect his baseball playing. He has dreamed of being on the all-star team, but now his guilty conscience is keeping him from playing well enough. How will Bus get over this? Read *All-Star Fever* to find out.

Great Lengths

Diersch, Sandra. James Lorimer & Co. Ltd., 1998. (IL 3–6, RL 5.2)

Do any of you play on a competitive team? Do you sometimes feel a lot of pressure to perform? Do you feel as if you let the coach down when you don't win? Is that a good feeling? Of course not. None of us like to fail. But what if you have so much pressure on you to win that you can't think of anything else? That's the way Jesse Cameron feels. She's the top swimmer on the team. There is a lot of pressure on her to win at all costs. Find out how the pressure gets to Jesse in *Great Lengths* by Sandra Diersch.

Soccer Shock

Napoli, Donna Jo. Puffin Books, 1991. (IL 3–6, RL 5.9)

Adam has one goal in mind—to make the soccer team. It is about all he thinks about. But does he even stand a chance of making the team? The coach yells at him all the time to pay more attention. Adam just knows he won't make the team. When he is walking home from practice, he is almost struck by lightning! He survives the experience but begins to hear strange voices. Can it be? Yes, his freckles are talking to him! Read *Soccer Shock* to find out what the freckles have to say!

There's a Girl in My Hammerlock
Spinelli, Jerry. Aladdin, 1993. (IL 5–8, RL 5.5)

A girl on the boys' wrestling team? It's unheard of. Why would eighth grader Maisie Potter even think of such a thing? She has a variety of reasons for wanting to be on the team. The coach isn't as enthusiastic as others about the prospect of having a girl on his squad. Some of the boys are openly hostile to Maisie. But Maisie is not a quitter. She works really hard to win a place on the team. Join Maisie as she sets out to achieve her goal.

Bat 6
Wolff, Virginia Euwer. Scholastic, 1998. (IL 5–8, RL 4.8)

Two teams get ready to meet for the 1949 Bat 6 championship. This is the 50th anniversary of the Barlow vs. Bear Creek sixth grade girls' baseball game. The tradition started in 1899 when the women of the two towns decided that they needed to mend some fences between the populations of the towns. The women played baseball and the men eventually began to talk to each other. The game evolved into a culminating event for the elementary school. In seventh grade, the girls would be going to school together at the Consolidated School, so this was a good time for the families to get together to enjoy the day. The teams each have some new girls in the sixth grade who make the team. What the towns cannot know is how these girls will change them forever. Join the girls from Barlow and Bear Creek Ridge as they spend their sixth grade lives getting ready for the big game. To find out what happens to the girls, read *Bat 6* by Virginia Euwer Wolff.

Axelrod, Amy. *Pigs on the Ball: Fun with Math and Sports*. Simon & Schuster Books for Young Readers, 1998. (IL K–3, RL 4.0) The Pig family visits a miniature golf course and learns about shapes, angles, and geometry.

Chardiet, Jon. *Parker Penguin and the Winter Games*. Scholastic, 1999. (IL K–3, RL 4.9) Even though his team is the worst in the school, Parker Penguin cares only about winning the Winter Games until his father shows him that winning isn't everything.

Dale, Jenny. *Spot the Sporty Puppy*. Aladdin Paperbacks, 2000. (IL K–3, RL 2.7) After getting in trouble for almost ruining Sports Day at Matt's school, Spot proves himself a hero.

Farrell, John. *It's Just a Game*. Caroline House/Boyds Mills Press, 1999. (IL K–3, RL 3.8) A soccer team learns that sports should be played not only to win but to have fun as well.

Herman, Gail. *Just Like Mike*. Delacorte Press, 2000. (IL K–3, RL 2.0) When Michael Brown's mother remarries and Michael's last name changes to Jordan, the kids at his new school expect him to be like his namesake on the basketball court, but unfortunately this Michael is terrible at sports.

Kennedy, X. J. *Elympics*. Philomel Books, 1999. (IL K–3, RL 3.0) Elephants compete in a variety of sports such as diving, triathlon, hammer throw, and figure skating.

LaMarche, Jim. *The Raft*. HarperCollins, 2000. (IL K–3, RL 2.2) Reluctant Nicky spends a wonderful summer with Grandma, who introduces him to the joy of rafting down the river near her home and watching the animals along the banks.

Santel, Mark. *Soccer Dreamin': The Golden Goal*. Eakin Press, 2000. (IL K–3, RL 3.3) Tommy is disappointed when his dream of scoring a goal for his soccer team does not happen in the way he had hoped, but his sister helps him see that there is more than one way to be a hero.

Swaim, Jessica. *Nate by Night*. Portunus, 2000. (IL K–3, RL 2.5) Dreaming of success in school, sports, and music lessons helps young Nate McTate find ways to make his dreams come true in real life.

Rey, Margret & H. A. *Curious George in the Snow*. Houghton Mifflin, 1998. (IL K–3, RL 4.3) A curious monkey causes quite a commotion on the ski slopes.

Alexander, Nina. *Alison Rides the Rapids*. Magic Attic Press, 1998. (IL 3–6, RL 5.7) When a disastrous math test shakes her self-confidence, Alison goes through the magic mirror and finds her skills and courage tested as a junior river guide on a whitewater rafting trip.

Christopher, Matt. *Hat Trick*. Little, Brown, 2000. (IL 3–6, RL 4.4) When Stookie's older brother gets his picture in the paper for scoring three goals in a soccer game, Stookie tries to emulate his feat.

Costello, Emily. *Foul Play*. Bantam, 1998. (IL 3–6, RL 3.3) Tess is looking forward to playing in her new soccer league, but she decides that if the team wants to win, she needs to get rid of the weaker players. Now her teammates must teach her that teamwork is more important than winning. Includes a section of soccer tips.

Crook, Marion. *Cutting It Close*. James Lorimer & Co. Ltd.; distributed by Orca Book Publishers, 1998. (IL 3–6, RL 6.0) Jayleen dreams of becoming Canada's greatest amateur barrel racer, but it seems her coach is against her for some reason Jayleen can't understand.

Hughes, Dean. *Bases Loaded*. Atheneum Books for Young Readers, 1999. (IL 3–6, RL 5.9) Because Gloria chews out her team members whenever they mess up, she sets the tone for infighting, which causes the coach to quit and leaves the future of the team in question.

Hughes, Dean. *Team Player*. Atheneum Books for Young Readers, 1999. (IL 3–6, RL 5.4) When Trent's best friend Robbie and another teammate on the Scrappers begin bragging about their baseball abilities, Trent worries that it will affect the team's play.

Krensky, Stephen. *Arthur Makes the Team*. Little, Brown, 1998. (IL 3–6, RL 2.8) Arthur really wants to play baseball on the Little League team with his friends, but when Francine teases him because he cannot seem to catch a ball, he worries that his skills are never going to be good enough.

Mantell, Paul. *Soccer Duel*. Little, Brown, 2000. (IL 3–6, RL 4.2) Team rivalry threatens to spoil a budding friendship between a showy soccer player, Bryce, and soft-spoken but talented Renny.

Swan, Bill. *Fast Finish*. James Lorimer & Co. Ltd.; distributed by Orca Book Publishers, 1999, 1998. (IL 3–6, RL 5.9) Noah is thrilled when he is asked to join the track team, but before he can succeed, he must overcome his past.

Activities (Grades K–3)

- Survey students about their favorite sport. How many are on teams? What sports are represented? How many enjoy watching games? Keep a chart. What is the most popular sport in your class?

- Tell students to write a letter to their favorite sports star that would include why they admire that person and what they believe makes him/her great.

- Lead the class in a discussion about the concept of being a good sport. Ask: What does this mean? Why is it important? How can you show that you are a good sport? How do you know when someone isn't a good sport?

- Teach students the rules of a new game. Hold a competition among different groups to play the new game.

- Have students makes up their own game. They should work in groups and use minimal equipment.

Activities (Grades 4–6)

- Survey the class to find out how many students participate in sports. Which sports are represented? What motivates the children to participate in sports?

- Lead the class in a discussion about the concept of "winning is everything." Ask: Is winning the only reason to participate in sports? Can you enjoy participating if you never win?

- Ask students to think about a time they felt like winners. This may or may not involve sports. Display student pictures and a paragraph about the winning experience.

- Most sports we hear about are traditional sports that have been around for a long time. Have students create a new sport or game of their own. They should work in groups. The game or sport should involve minimal equipment.

- Instruct students to research their favorite sport. The students should learn about the history of the sport, its rules, and how widespread it is. Students could share the information via a PowerPoint presentation.

Westward Expansion

When we think of pioneers, we think of covered wagons making their way west. We think of sturdy people leaving everything behind to start a new life. We might even envision Laura Ingalls and her family living on the prairie. These books show different views of the journey west. Children will understand what it took to travel to a new home. They will gain insight into what life was like for children in the 1800s. How many children today could even imagine being without a computer, television, or telephone?

Booktalks (Grades K–3)

Nine for California

Levitin, Sonia; ill. by Cat Bowman Smith. Orchard Books, 1996. (IL K–3, RL 2.8)

Young Amanda is so excited when her mother receives a letter from their pa telling them to join him in California. He had gone out the year before to work the gold mines. Now, the family will make the journey to join him. It will take 21 days by stagecoach. Everything is packed—including a big flour sack that Mama has packed. "What's in the sack, Mama?" the children all want to know. Mama just tells them that it is everything they will need for their journey. Find out what adventures await them and just what is in Mama's sack in *Nine for California.*

Roughing It on the Oregon Trail

Stanley, Diane; ill. by Holly Berry. Joanna Cotler Books, 2000. (IL K–3, RL 3.0)

Liz and Lenny don't have any idea of what to expect when they go to stay with their grandmother while their parents are away. Grandma loves to find out things about their ancestors, and her home is filled with pictures of family from long ago. When she asks them which of their ancestors they would like to visit, Liz and Lenny pick their great-great-great-great-grandmother. Little do they realize that Grandma can transport them back in time to meet her! Before they know it, they are back in 1843 joining a wagon train setting out for Oregon. They spend 5 weeks sharing a wagon with their ancestors and finding out what their life was like on the Oregon Trail. It took a special kind of person to endure the long trip out west with no highways or modern transportation. Read Diane Stanley's book if you would like to know what it was like *Roughing It on the Oregon Trail.*

Dakota Dugout

Turner, Ann; ill. by Ronald Himler. Aladdin Books, 1985. (IL K–3, RL 3.4)

Tell you about what my life was like on the prairie? I'd love to. Talking about it brings it back to me as if it was yesterday. I'll tell you what it was like to live in a house made of dirt. I'll tell you about how alone you feel out on the prairie. I'll tell you about our hopes and dreams as we watched the corn grow tall in the summer. I'll also tell you about how I felt when it all changed. I'll tell you all about my *Dakota Dugout*.

Going West

Van Leeuwen, Jean; ill. by Thomas B. Allen. Dial Books for Young Readers, 1992. (IL K–3, RL 4.5)

Blankets and pillows and quilts, Mama's favorite rocking chair, trunks full of clothes, barrels full of food, a cook stove, a box of tin dishes, all of Mama's cooking pots, all of Papa's tools, a Bible, a rifle, and a spinning wheel. This is all Hannah's family packed in the covered wagon when they set off to find a new home. They left their comfortable home in the East to find a new life in the prairie. When the family finally arrived, Hannah could not believe that this lonely place was the home her father longed for. Join Hannah and her family as they make a place for themselves in a new land. They are *Going West*.

Summertime In the Big Woods.

Wilder, Laura Ingalls; ill. by Renee Graef. HarperCollins, 1996. (IL K–3, RL 3.9)

Have you heard of the Little House on the Prairie series by Laura Ingalls Wilder? She wrote about her life growing up in the 1800s. Her books follow the family's adventures going west to find a better life. This book is an adaptation of one of her books. Can someone tell me what an adaptation is? It means that this is not the original book but has been rewritten in another form—in this case, a form to help younger readers enjoy Laura's stories. This book tells of the Ingalls girls' life in the big woods of Wisconsin. We find out about their summer chores and how they spend their days. Join the girls as they visit neighbors, help Ma make cheese, and help Pa with the dripping golden honeycombs from the bee tree. Spend *Summertime In the Big Woods* by Laura Ingalls Wilder.

Booktalks (Grades 4–6)

Across the Wide and Lonesome Prairie: The Oregon Trail Diary of Hattie Campbell (Dear America Series).

Gregory, Kristiana. Scholastic, 1997. (IL 5–8, RL 5.2)

Hattie Campbell and her family are traveling to Oregon in 1847. This story is told through Hattie's diary entries. "We live through bad weather, disease, and death. We witness the good times as well as the bad times." The story follows Hattie all through the 8-month journey to a new life in the West. Ride with Hattie *Across the Wide and Lonesome Prairie: The Oregon Trail Diary of Hattie Campbell*.

The Gentleman Outlaw and Me—Eli: A Story of the Old West

Hahn, Mary Downing. Clarion, 1996. (IL 5–8, RL 4.6)

Twelve-year-old Eliza Yates wants to join her father in the silver mines of Colorado. Her mother has died and she is left with mean relatives in Kansas. She decides to run away to try to find her father. Along the way, she decides that it will be easier to travel if she were a boy. So she cuts her hair, puts on overalls and a hat, and begins to call herself Eli. She soon meets up with Calvin Featherbone, who calls himself Gentleman Outlaw. Calvin is off to Colorado to avenge his own father's death at the hands of Sheriff Alfred Yates, Eliza's father. The adventures these two share along the way are truly funny. Calvin is always cooking up schemes that are doomed from the start. If you enjoy funny stories with an Old West setting, *The Gentleman Outlaw and Me—Eli* is sure to entertain.

Jason's Gold

Hobbs, Will. Morrow Junior Books, 1999. (IL 5–8, RL 5.1)

Young Jason Hawthorne is on his way to the Klondike region near Alaska. He hears there is a huge gold strike up there, so he travels from New York City to meet up with his brothers in Seattle, where a small inheritance awaits him. Jason plans to ask his brothers to finance his trip north. He's in for a big surprise when he gets to Seattle only to find his brothers had the same idea. They left with his money to strike it rich in the Klondike, and they have about a four-day head start on him. Jason sets out to meet up with them. It's a hard journey—especially with no money. Jason has a long, hard adventure in front of him, but the people he meets along the way are well worth the trouble. Join Jason as he sets out to find *Jason's Gold*.

The Great Turkey Walk

Karr, Kathleen. Farrar, Straus & Giroux, 1998. (IL 3–6, RL 4.8)

Have you ever heard of the great cattle drives? Cowboys would round up a herd of cattle and have them walk long distances. This was the only way to deliver cattle to their destination before trains were in use. This story takes place in 1860. Simon Green is 15 years old and is graduating from school. His teacher sends him out in the world with the advice to spread his wings. Simon gets a great idea. At least it sounds like a great idea at the time. He buys 1,000 turkeys and sets off to deliver them from Missouri to Denver. And you know how he needs to do it? That's right, he walks them all the way. He sets off with 1,000 turkeys, a wagonload of corn, two mules, and an old man to drive the turkeys. Will they make it the whole way? Will the journey be uneventful? You just know this has to be a very funny story, don't you? Have a laugh while reading *The Great Turkey Walk* by Kathleen Karr.

Sarah, Plain and Tall

MacLachlan, Patricia. Harper & Row, 1985. (IL 3–6, RL 3.9)

Jacob lives on the prairie with his children. His wife died years before when Caleb was born. Jacob decides that the children need a new mother. But how do you find a wife when you live on the prairie in the 1800s? A common practice is to place an ad in the newspapers back east and find a mail order bride. This is just what Jacob decides to do. One lady who writes back is from Maine. She tells Jacob that she is quite tall and not very pretty. She's just plain and tall. They write several times, and then he invites her to visit. She agrees and decides to spend the summer. The children come to love Sarah, but Jacob is not very friendly. Sarah misses the ocean terribly. When Sarah goes to town by herself, Jacob and the children are afraid that she has decided to return to Maine. Jacob realizes how much he cares for her. Will he be able to tell Sarah or will she return to Maine? To find out, read *Sarah, Plain and Tall* by Patricia MacLachlan.

Book List (Grades K–3)

Ackerman, Karen. *Araminta's Paint Box*. Aladdin Paperbacks, 1998. (IL K–3, RL 4.5) When her family moves from Boston to California in 1847, Araminta and her paint box become separated, but through a series of new owners, the paint box finds its way to California.

Bunting, Eve. *Dandelions*. Harcourt Brace, 1995. (IL K–3, RL 3.1) Zoe and her family find strength in each other as they make a new home in the Nebraska territory.

Gerrard, Roy. *Wagons West!* Farrar, Straus & Giroux, 1996. (IL K–3, RL 3.9) A rhyming story of a family's move by wagon train from Missouri to Oregon in the 1850s and their daughter's role in outwitting cattle thieves.

Harper, Jo. *Prairie Dog Pioneers*. Turtle Books, 1998. (IL K–3, RL 3.9) Because Mae Dean misinterprets her father's actions while journeying to their new home on the Texas prairie, she begins to feel that he doesn't care for her anymore.

Hutchins, H. J. *Tess*. Annick Press. (IL K–3, RL 4.8) The story of Tess, a young girl who loves her prairie home—even when she has to gather cow-patties for fuel—and the good deed that earns her the respect of a grumpy neighbor.

Karim, Roberta. *Kindle Me a Riddle: A Pioneer Story*. Greenwillow Books, 1999. (IL K–3, RL 4.3) The riddles that a pioneer family share explain the origin of such things in their lives as their log cabin, johnnycakes, the broom, a cloak, candles, and more.

Levitin, Sonia. *Boom Town*. Orchard Books, 1998. (IL K–3, RL 3.5) After her family moves to California where her father goes to work in the gold fields, Amanda decides to make her own fortune baking pies. She encourages others to provide the necessary services—from a general store to a school—that enable her town to prosper.

Sanders, Scott R. *Aurora Means Dawn*. Aladdin Paperbacks, 1998. (IL K–3, RL 3.3) After traveling from Connecticut to Ohio in 1800 to start a new life in the settlement of Aurora, the Sheldons find that they are the first family to arrive there and realize that they will be starting a new community by themselves.

Stutson, Caroline. *Prairie Primer: A to Z*. Puffin Books, 1999. (IL K–3, RL 2.5) Life on the prairie is depicted in this rhyming alphabet book.

Trottier, Maxine. *Prairie Willow*. Stoddart Kids, 1998. (IL K–3, RL 3.5) Emily, a young girl who has moved with her family to the vast, open prairie, plants a willow tree on the farm that grows along with her throughout her life and beyond.

Book List (Grades 4–6)

Fritz, Jean. *The Cabin Faced West*. Puffin Books, 1987. (IL 3–6, RL 4.5) Ten-year-old Ann overcomes loneliness and learns to appreciate the importance of her role in settling the wilderness of western Pennsylvania.

Kudlinski, Kathleen V. *Facing West: A Story of the Oregon Trail*. Puffin Books, 1996. (IL 3–6, RL 2.5) As his family sets out from Missouri to Oregon, young Ben wonders whether he will have more trouble with the dangers of the journey or his debilitating asthma.

Kurtz, Jane. *I'm Sorry, Almira Ann*. Holt, 1999. (IL 3–6, RL 3.0) Eight-year-old Sarah's high spirits help make her family's long journey from Missouri to Oregon more bearable, though they do cause both her and her best friend Almira Ann some problems.

Little, Jean. *The Belonging Place*. Viking, 1997. (IL 3–6, RL 3.5) Elspet Mary is happy to be living with her kind aunt and uncle after her mother and father die, but she worries when the family decides to go to Upper Canada from Scotland to settle their own farm.

Love, D. Anne. *Bess's Log Cabin Quilt*. Holiday House, 1995. (IL 3–6, RL 4.8) With her father away and her mother ill with fever, 10-year-old Bess works hard on a log cabin quilt to save the family farm.

MacLachlan, Patricia. *Skylark*. HarperTrophy, 1997. (IL 3–6, RL 3.3) When a drought tests the commitment of a mail-order bride from Maine to her new home on the prairie, her stepchildren hope they will be able to remain a family.

Moss, Marissa. *Rachel's Journal: The Story of a Pioneer Girl*. Silver Whistle/Harcourt Brace, 1998. (IL 3–6, RL 5.2) In her journal, Rachel chronicles her family's adventures traveling by covered wagon on the Oregon Trail in 1850.

Reynolds, Marilynn. *The New Land: A First Year on the Prairie*. Orca Book Publishers, 1999. (IL 3–6, RL 4.8) A family journeys overseas to the American West, where they build a homestead, plant crops, and begin their new lives.

Wilder, Laura Ingalls. *Little House on the Prairie*. HarperTrophy, 1971. (IL 3–6, RL 4.3) Laura Ingalls and her family move to Indian country in frontier Kansas.

Woodruff, Elvira. *Dear Levi: Letters from the Overland Trail*. Knopf, 1998. (IL 3–6, RL 4.9) Twelve-year-old Austin Ives writes letters to his younger brother describing his 3,000-mile journey from their home in Pennsylvania to Oregon in 1851.

Activities (Grades K–3)

- Lead students in a discussion about moving to a new place to start over. The brave people who left their homes could only take a limited amount of belongings on their journey. Brainstorm a list of things you would take. Ask: What are the essentials? Which are personal? If you could only take one of your personal belongings, what would you take and why?

- There were no supermarkets or convenience stores along the way west. When the pioneers reached their destination, there were most often alone and had to be self-sufficient. They made their own clothes and grew their own food. One food they made was butter. Help the children make their own butter. Begin with empty baby food jars; add a few tablespoons of heavy cream. Place the covers securely on the jars. Students can then shake the jars vigorously for about 15 minutes. They should see a lump of butter formed in the jar. The liquid in the jar is buttermilk, which was used in many ways. Have the children spread their butter on crackers for a pioneer treat. Ask the children if they would rather have to make their butter every time or just buy it at the store!

- Create a word search using the website Puzzlemaker.com at *http://puzzlemaker.com*. Include terms learned from the books about pioneer life, such as covered wagon, log cabin, johnnycakes, broom, cloak, and candles.

- Help students research prairie plants and animals and create a poster illustrating the species they've found.

- Children of the pioneers didn't have a lot of toys to play with. Most of the games they played needed very little equipment. Have the children play some pioneer games. Drop the Handkerchief is much like today's Duck Duck Goose. Children sit in a circle facing inward. The child who is "it" walks around the back of the children and drops the handkerchief on one child, who must then catch the first child before that child runs the complete circle and sits in the second child's place. Leapfrog was another popular pioneer game. Croquet is one pioneer game that used sporting equipment. If you can secure the loan of a croquet set, the children can learn to play this game.

Activities (Grades 4–6)

- It took a special type of person to become a pioneer. Help students brainstorm some of the characteristics or motivations that contributed to this westward movement, such as a sense of adventure, dreams of a better future, and the desire to have more land.

- Ask students to pretend that they have taken the journey west and have finally arrived in their new home. They can write a letter to those back east describing the journey and their new home.

- Have students create a diorama of a wagon train heading west. What do the wagons look like? Are all the people riding in the wagons? What types of animals are pulling the wagons? What other animals are traveling with the families?

- Have students make a poster that tells about the plants and animals the families would encounter on their journey.

- When families made their homes out west, they needed to be quite independent, making their own clothes, growing their own food, and even creating their own entertainment. Toys were homemade and often crude. Help students create their own cornhusk dolls. Directions can be found at *www.ontariocorn.org/husk2.html*.